PALESTINE IN PERSPECTIVE

PALESTINE IN PERSPECTIVE

Politics, Human Rights & the West Bank

David H. Ott

QUARTET BOOKS

LONDON   MELBOURNE   NEW YORK

First published by Quartet Books Limited 1980
A member of the Namara Group
27/29 Goodge Street, London W1P 1FD

Copyright © 1980 by David H. Ott

ISBN 0 7043 2263 3

Printed in Great Britain at The Anchor Press Ltd
and bound by Wm Brendon & Son Ltd,
both of Tiptree, Essex

To Rihab
without whom it would never have been

Contents

Acknowledgements

This work's first incarnation was as my LL.M. thesis at Harvard Law School where Professor Richard Baxter, as he then was, guided my steps along the pathways of International Law. To him must go prime thanks for his unfailing help and encouragement then and since.

Gordon Bonnyman, an eager champion of justice in Jerusalem and elsewhere, contributed an inspiring example and a number of ideas that have found their way into these pages.

To Jim and Debbie Fine go much appreciation for their faith and for their vigorous efforts to foster reconciliation in Palestine.

On the West Bank friends and colleagues whom it would be unwise to name have played their part over many years in upholding humanitarian values, in the process giving an impetus to the completion of this book. My admiration for their physical and moral courage is unbounded.

Ann Lesch deserves special mention for her enthusiastic interest in this project as in all things Middle Eastern.

Thanks are due also to Michael Adams for his kind assistance to an almost total stranger.

Appreciation is extended to Dennis Skiotis who over several years saw to it that I could pursue that interest in Middle Eastern studies which underlies much of this work.

My new-found colleagues in Aberdeen have offered a warm welcome to the outlandish arrival in their midst and (dare one say it?) canny advice to a novice author. Professor Frank Lyall's counsel and support have been unstinting and highly productive, and Alison Seager's amiable patience has often seemed saintly.

Eileen Carr shepherded my draft through its final typing with her usual sparkle and good humour. Audrey Noble, Carol Brown, Fiona Chaplain, and Elaine MacKenzie exhausted miles of typewriter ribbon in a furious (and successful) effort to meet a deadline.

Tolerating the intolerable, my family at some sacrifice to themselves provided a haven wherein this work could metamorphose into its ultimate form. They have my gratitude for their loyalty and generosity.

DAVID H. OTT

University of Aberdeen,
July 1980

Introduction

As a result of the Arab-Israeli war of June 1967, Israeli armed forces gained control of the Palestinian-populated territories of the West Bank (formerly under Jordanian administration) and the Gaza Strip (formerly under Egyptian administration). Under international law, both areas, pending legitimate alteration of their status, were subject to Israeli military government during the period of what is technically styled belligerent occupation. The rights and duties of all parties in a situation of belligerent occupation are governed and determined by international law, and in particular by the Hague Regulations of 1907 and the Fourth Geneva Convention of 1949. Relevant provisions of these documents will be examined in detail in the course of this study, since they provide the legal framework within which involved parties adhering to the requirements of international law must act.

Interminable belligerent occupation of the two territories has generally been seen as undesirable, and proposals for regularizing their status have been put forward. On December 28, 1977, Israeli Prime Minister Menachem Begin read to the Israeli Knesset the text of a detailed plan (hereinafter, the Begin Plan) suggesting some measure of Palestinian 'self-rule' or 'autonomy' in the West Bank and the Gaza Strip. Subsequently, at the Camp David summit of President Jimmy Carter, President Anwar Sadat of Egypt, and Prime Minister Begin, the three parties agreed on

1

September 17, 1978 to 'A Framework for Peace in the Middle East'. Section A of that document outlined a three-stage process of negotiations relating to the territories. In conjunction with the signing of the Egyptian-Israeli Peace Treaty of March 26, 1979, the two nations agreed, in a letter from Messrs Sadat and Begin to Mr Carter, to proceed with negotiations to implement the West Bank-Gaza provisions of the Framework. On May 21, 1979, the Israeli Cabinet added significant supplementary amendments to the Begin Plan and agreed that the amended Begin Plan (hereinafter, the Plan) should serve as the guidelines for Israel's representatives in the negotiations under the Framework.

In analyzing the documents produced at these stages in the discussions of what has come to be called 'Palestinian autonomy', one must bear in mind that each document derives some of its current significance from its relationship to the others. This is particularly true of the Begin Plan and the amendments of May 1979. The latter, for example, clarified the Begin Plan's position on sovereignty, while the Begin Plan's provision for 'security and public order' illuminated the amendment dealing with the role of the 'Israeli security services'. Hence, a strict chronological study has been rejected in favour of a topical analysis of the basic Israeli proposals, and some of their later ramifications. In addition, because these proposals have become part of a broader legal and political debate, it has been considered appropriate to examine also reasonable alternative arrangements for the West Bank and Gaza.

This study adopts throughout the perspective of public international law as that most suitable for bringing to bear the highest generally-accepted standards of international behaviour.

The book considers the period up to December 31, 1979, although it has been possible to include developments beyond that date in some instances.

1 The Israeli Autonomy Plan and the Question of Sovereignty

Outline of the Plan

The Begin Plan of December 1977 expressed an intention to bestow what it termed 'administrative autonomy' on the Arab population of the West Bank and the Gaza Strip[1] while maintaining responsibility for 'security and public order' in the hands of the 'Israeli authorities' and permitting residents of Israel to acquire land and settle in those territories.[2] The Palestinian residents of the area would be allowed to choose either Israeli or Jordanian citizenship[3] and to participate in the political life of the country whose citizenship was chosen.[4] An Administrative Council, elected by voting in which all residents of the areas 'without distinction of citizenship'[5] would participate, but exercising responsibility only for affairs of the Arab Palestinians amongst those inhabitants,[6] would operate departments concerned with a variety of matters including education, refugee rehabilitation, and 'the administration of justice and the supervision of the local police forces'.[7] Various committees with representatives from Israel, Jordan and the Administrative Council would be formed to deal with particular aspects of the Plan's implementation,[8] and the Administrative Council would appoint 'one of its members' (who may be elected from any of the population groups resident in the areas[9]) to represent it before the Government of Israel and one of its members to perform the same task with regard to the Government of Jordan.[10] The Begin Plan 'proposes ... that the question of

3

sovereignty [in these areas] be left open',[11] and it envisaged review after a five-year period.[12]

The supplementary amendments given Israeli Cabinet approval on May 21, 1979,[13] added important new elements to the Begin Plan. Close analysis of the latter could have led to the conclusion that Israel intended to assert sovereignty over the occupied territories. In approving the May amendments the Cabinet did in fact endorse a declaration that Israel would claim sovereignty at the end of the five-year period.[14] This clarification serves to emphasize that nothing in the Begin Plan conflicted with a future Israeli claim of sovereignty and much in it positively promoted Israeli sovereignty by enhancing and consolidating the sovereign-like powers already temporarily accorded Israel as belligerent occupant. The pervasive significance of this aspect of the Plan's proposals will be apparent as this study proceeds.

The Cabinet approval of May 1979 extended also to provisions that:

> Whereas water resources affect the entire area and will require regional planning, Israel will be responsible for planning water administration;
> Jewish settlers would remain under Israeli jurisdiction;
> The struggle against terror, subversion and violence of any kind will remain in the hands of the Israeli security services.[15]

Uncultivated government-owned land, land not legally registered in private ownership but cultivated by Palestinians, as well as cultivated and uncultivated Palestinian-owned land, would all, in varying degrees, be subject to Israeli control and use.[16]

A majority of the Cabinet was reported to favour the proposition that the authority of an Arab autonomous administration should derive solely from the Israeli military government, whose continuance had already been recommended by the Ben-Elissar interministerial committee on autonomy.[17]

Undoubtedly the most important of these new positions was that indicating the military government would continue and that declaring Israel's intention to assert sovereignty over the territories. The implications of each must be considered preliminarily at this point.

There is no inconsistency between the intention in Article 1 of the Begin Plan to abolish the administration of the military government and the more recent indication that the military government itself would continue in existence. Furthermore, changes in the structure of the occupation regime would not terminate the occupation since, in the situation prevailing in the West Bank and Gaza, termination could only be accomplished by complete Israeli withdrawal, by liberation, or by treaty.[18] Autonomy under the Plan would therefore remain well within the following legal description of occupation government:

> The occupant may, while retaining its paramount authority, permit the government of the country to perform some or all of its normal functions ... Such action is consistent with the status of occupation, so long as there exists the firm possession and the purpose to maintain paramount authority.
>
> It is immaterial whether the government over an enemy's territory consists in a military or civil or mixed administration. Its character is the same and the source of its authority the same. *It is a government imposed by force, and the legality of its acts is determined by the law of war.*[19] [emphasis supplied]

In the sense used here, 'the law of war' includes that of belligerent occupation, particularly the Hague Regulations of 1907 and the Fourth Geneva Convention of 1949.[20] Under this law

> [t]he basic duty of the occupant is to preserve the existing situation in the occupied territories. Only minimal changes essential and unavoidable for the maintenance of military security* and the preservation of the public order and welfare of the inhabitants are permitted. The operative premise of such regulation is that other changes may not only be directly inimical to the best interests of the population but make more difficult the peace-making process by creating vested interests in the maintenance of occupation.[21]

This is the standard, with its attendant rights and duties under

---

* The nature and extent of what is permitted by 'military necessity', the international legal concept applicable to questions of 'military security', are considered in detail in Chapter 3, below.

5

international law, by which the Israeli autonomy scheme's arrangements must be judged.

Israel's Assertion of Sovereignty

Although Israel's intention to claim sovereignty may have been published as a Cabinet declaration in order to suggest that Israel considered this issue settled and non-negotiable, it must nevertheless be a main point of contention, given the political realities of the Middle East. Sovereignty is indeed the ground-bass over which the diapason of the Plan's proposals is played. Furthermore, the question of sovereignty will be seen to be at the centre of the conflict between Israel and the Palestinians. The resulting importance of the subject justifies an examination of the concept in international law.

Sovereignty in International Law

Since the Plan as published contains no definitions of its terms, it is appropriate to consider the spectrum of meanings that international law attaches to the word 'sovereignty'. This range has been concisely stated in a standard treatise:

> Sovereignty as supreme authority, which is independent of any other earthly authority, may be said to have different aspects. Inasmuch as it excludes dependence upon any other authority, and in particular from the authority of another State, sovereignty is *independence*. It is *external* independence with regard to the liberty of action outside its borders in the intercourse with other States which a State enjoys. It is *internal* independence with regard to the liberty of action of a State inside its borders. As comprising the power of a State to exercise supreme authority over all persons and things within its territory, sovereignty is *territorial* supremacy (*dominium, territorial sovereignty*). As comprising the power of a State to exercise supreme authority over its citizens at home and abroad, sovereignty is *personal* supremacy (*imperium, political sovereignty*).[22] [emphasis in the original]

Thus sovereignty may be broadly understood to apply on the one hand to the status of a state vis-à-vis other states (i.e. 'external/internal independence') and on the other hand to the nature and extent of a state's power and authority within its sphere of exclusivity (i.e. 'territorial/political supremacy'). While the two aspects of independence are essentially two sides of the same coin, the relationship between the two facets of supremacy is perhaps less clear. The Latin nomenclature suggests a distinction between powers of 'ownership' (*dominium*) and the power to command (*imperium*).[23] Are these two facets on an equal footing in law? It would appear that they are not. For, while the existence of territory under control like that implied in 'ownership' may be taken as a criterion of statehood,[24] a state's power to command its citizens abroad would seem derivative from the existence of statehood. Territorial supremacy would thus precede, and lay the basis for, political supremacy. Put in another way, political supremacy would not exist without prior supremacy over territory. As one treatise puts it, the 'so-called external jurisdiction of the state is, in fact, only a limited expression of state authority, which in substance follows from its exclusive power over state territory'.[25]

The concept of 'ownership' (*dominium*) of course implies more than the mere exercise of control, for it raises also issues of title relating to

(1) why the competence [to control] exists and what its fullest possible extent may be;
(2) whether claims may be enforced in respect of interference with the territorial aspects of that competence ...
The second aspect mentioned is the essence of title: the validity of claims to territorial sovereignty against other states ... In principle the concept of ownership, opposable to all other states and unititular, can and does exist in international law ... However, in practice the concept of title employed to solve disputes approximates to the notion of the better right to possess familiar in the Common law.[26]

Logic suggests that questions of validity of title (i.e. of the right to 'ownership') are fundamentally prerequisite to other questions of territorial supremacy which would be relevant only after valid title had been established.

Sovereignty and the Plan

Thus it is possible to say initially that 'the question of sovereignty' in the Plan involves, at a minimum, state independence on the one

7

hand and title and legal power as aspects of territorial supremacy on the other.

By leaving open the question of sovereignty-as-independence, the Begin Plan would in effect propose a present agreement between the parties involved that in the future they would make no claims for, nor recognize, an independent entity in the affected territories. This follows necessarily from application of the Begin Plan's formula to territories not now independent. For not to decide on independence for dependent territories is in effect to decide that they should not be independent. The parties would be called on positively to reject independence, at least initially, by accepting the present situation. This would further the attainment of one goal of current Israeli policy by gaining general, and Arab, acquiescence in Israel's refusal to countenance a Palestinian state 'in Eretz Israel'.[27] The Palestinians would then be at best temporarily precluded from establishing an independent statehood which would embody their territorial supremacy over the territories. Israel, however, would be free as far as the Plan is concerned to use its own pre-existing independent status as a legal base from which to extend and develop Israeli territorial sovereignty over the areas.

This leads to the ultimate significance of Israel's publicly declared intention to claim 'sovereignty' at the end of the interim period: Israel would assert territorial supremacy. As indicated above, such an assertion would raise issues of title and of the nature and extent of the sovereign's powers. As will be seen, the Plan touches directly on the preliminary manifestations of these issues by providing for the exclusivity or the supremacy, or both, of Israel's position at the centre of the proposed autonomy arrangements.

Two further questions then arise: by what right can Israel claim such a position? and, what are the legal implications of arrangements aiming to confirm that position?

Close examination of the Plan's provisions in the light of international law will help to elucidate these intertwined issues and questions.

NOTES

1   The Begin Plan, Article 2. The Begin Plan is reproduced in the Appendix.

2   *Id*. Arts. 11 and 20.
3   *Id*. Art. 14.
4   *Id*. Arts. 16–17.
5   *Id*. Art. 4.
6   *Id*. Art. 9.
7   *Id*. Art. 10.
8   *Id*. Art. 19, 21.
9   *Id*. Art. 5.
10 *Id*. Art. 23.
11 *Id*. Art. 24; *see* Appendix, 'Note'.
12 *Id*. Art. 26.
13 N.Y. Times, May 22, 1979, p.1, col.1.
14 *Id*.
15 N.Y. Times, May 9, 1979, p. A 11, col.1.
16 The Jerusalem Post Int'l Ed., May 20–26, 1979.
17 N.Y. Times, May 18, 1979, p.1, cols. 4 & 5; N.Y. Times, Feb. 10, 1979, p.4, col.6.
18 VON GLAHN, LAW AMONG NATIONS 688 (3rd ed.).
19 United States Department of the Army, FIELD MANUAL ON THE LAW OF LAND WARFARE (FM 27–10) (1956) at 141–142, Paragraphs 367, 368.
20 The Hague Regulations are an Annexe to the Convention on the Laws and Customs of War on land, *signed* Oct. 18, 1907, 36 Stat. 2277, T.S. No. 539. The Fourth Geneva Convention is the Convention Relative to the Protection of Civilian Persons in Time of War, Aug. 12, 1949, 6 U.S.T. 3516, T.I.A.S. No. 3365, 75 U.N.T.S. 287.
21 GERSON, ISRAEL, THE WEST BANK AND INTERNATIONAL LAW 170.
22 L. OPPENHEIM, I INTERNATIONAL LAW 286 (8th ed. Sir H. Lauterpacht, editor). Hereinafter, this work will be cited as I LAUTERPACHT–OPPENHEIM.
23 Cf. BLACK'S LAW DICTIONARY (4th ed.), *sub voc.* 'DOMINIUM' and 'IMPERIUM'.
24 Cf. BROWNLIE, PRINCIPLES OF PUBLIC INTERNATIONAL LAW 74–75 (3rd ed.). Hereinafter cited as BROWNLIE PUBLIC.
25 Sahovic & Bishop, 'The Authority of the State: Its Range with respect to Persons and Places', in MANUAL OF PUBLIC INTERNATIONAL LAW 311, at 317, (ed. Max Sørensen). Hereinafter, the MANUAL will be cited as

SØRENSEN

26 BROWNLIE PUBLIC, note 24 *supra*, at 126.
27 Jerusalem Post Int'l Ed. June 28, 1977, p.5, col.1. On May 21, 1979, the Israeli Cabinet approved a declaration that Israel would forever oppose establishment of a Palestinian state. N.Y. Times, May 22, 1979, p.1, col.1.

2 Israel's Territorial Supremacy under the Plan: Veto Power, Extraterritoriality, Water Resources, Land

To understand Israeli supremacy under the Plan it is helpful to consider first the roles assigned to the two other prospective partners in the Israeli autonomy scheme.

The Administrative Council to be established under Article 3 of the 1977 Begin Plan is clearly in a subordinate position. It would lack ultimate or exclusive authority for all persons and things within the territories and would instead have under its direction and within its competence only those 'administrative affairs relating to the Arab residents' of the areas.[1] The Council would thus be denied legislative powers[2] and would not be given any responsibility for the affairs of non-Arabs. In terms of the functions of the Council, autonomy would indeed be, as Israeli policy makers insist, for the people and not for the land,[3] that is, would have an ethnic, and not a geographical, reference.

Jordan, which according to the Begin Plan would permit Palestinians choosing Jordanian citizenship to vote, and stand as candidates, in Jordanian parliamentary elections,[4] would not exercise exclusive authority even on this matter. For Article 18 requires that '[q]uestions arising from the vote' be 'clarified' in negotiations between Israel and Jordan. Nor would Jordan have exclusive control over applicable legislation within the territories[5] or 'immigration' of refugees into the areas[6] but rather would in both matters share power with the Administrative Council and Israel.

The role assigned to Israel under the Plan is, however, significantly more powerful and, it is submitted, gives Israel effective *de facto* territorial supremacy.

Israel's Veto Power

Articles 19 and 21 effectively establish the power of the veto by requiring unanimity in decisions of the tripartite committees responsible for reaffirming or abolishing existing legislation and for determining the norms of Palestinian 'immigration' into the affected areas. The veto impinges on Israel quite differently, however, than on the other partners. For the effect of the veto would be that, failing unanimity, no changes could be introduced into the existing situation prevailing at the time the Plan entered into force. The nature of that situation could be influenced to a considerable extent by prior decisions of the Israeli military administration during the period of the occupation.[7] Israel could thus theoretically form and then maintain that situation pretty much as she wished it to be while the other partners could effect no changes without Israel's consent.

Extraterritoriality

Concerned as it was with 'the administrative affairs relating to the Arab residents',[8] the Begin Plan was silent on the legal position of Jews living in the territories. Yet it was possible to deduce even from the Begin Plan an assumption of a special status for those Jews. The amendments of May 1979 confirmed that Israel would demand that Jewish settlers should remain under Israeli jurisdiction.[9] Since it would seem unnecessary (and rather uncharacteristic) of Israel to seek foreign approval (through acceptance of the Plan) of the unquestionable right of Israel, as a sovereign state, to exercise traditional personal supremacy over her own nationals, it may reasonably be inferred that the Plan intends to go further and stretch Israeli jurisdiction into the territories to encompass all legal matters in which Jews are involved. This may accurately be referred to as extraterritorial jurisdiction, i.e., 'jurisdiction exercised by a nation in other countries'.[10] The resulting restriction on the Administrative

Council's jurisdiction recalls the limitations imposed on the sovereignty of the former Ottoman Empire by the Capitulations. Under these agreements on extraterritoriality, the representatives of Western governments exercized, on Ottoman soil, 'complete civil and criminal jurisdiction'[11] over their nationals in Ottoman territory. Ottoman courts under these arrangements were limited to cases between Ottoman subjects only, and disputes in which both Ottoman subjects and foreign parties were involved were not heard by Ottoman courts but rather were put to arbitration in which diplomatic or other pressures could overbear the Ottoman subject's legal rights.[12] One scholar has concluded that

> the vagueness and empiricism of extraterritoriality were such that its true content tended to reflect, not the principles it rested on, but rather the balance of power between the local government and the foreign residents.[13]

The possible capitulatory restrictions that extraterritoriality could place on the Council's authority are emphasized by the Plan's position on the basic question of the Council's continuing in operation the present indigenous judicial system. The language of Article 10 of the Begin Plan, providing for a Council department responsible for the 'administration of justice and the supervision of the local police forces', is ambiguous. 'Administration of justice' in the context of a single department responsible also for the police forces suggests a combining of police and prison administration in one Council portfolio, as in the Israeli Ministry of Police. By this reading, the Plan would make no provision for a court system under the Council.[14] Only Israeli courts, civil or military, would then be available.

But, even assuming that Article 10 aims to continue the indigenous court system, would indigenous and Israeli courts find themselves in competition or confrontation? Extraterritoriality, implicitly reserving exclusively to Israeli courts large areas of jurisdiction, might avoid this problem, but only at the expense of Palestinian rights.

For, apart from criminal jurisdiction, the indigenous Council courts would normally be expected to have jurisdiction over commercial and land questions on the civil side. In the nature of the political and economic situation in the territories, precisely these types of cases would be most likely to involve not exclusively Palestinians but Jews as well. Yet the Council, and by extension

13

its courts, would have jurisdiction only over Arabs and Arab affairs. Autonomy for the people but not the land would withhold from the Council's courts a geographical basis for jurisdiction over Jews within the territories. But Jewish extraterritoriality, as part of the Plan, would go further and explicitly remove Jews altogether from any but Israeli jurisdiction. The Council's courts would therefore not be authorized to hear any cases in which Jews were parties. The consequent inability of Palestinians to obtain in their own court's judgement against Jews who would be subject to the jurisdiction of Israeli courts would no doubt decrease rivalry between the two court systems. But, more significantly, it would also mean that, in potentially important suits in which the Palestinians of the territories could normally expect to seek legal remedies in their own courts, they would find themselves denied access.

This limitation would effectively abolish in the indigenous courts, as between Arabs and Jews, causes of action which the Palestinian inhabitants would otherwise have under their present indigenous legal regime. Abolition would contravene Article 23 of the Hague Regulations[15] forbidding the occupant from declaring 'abolished, suspended, or inadmissible in a Court of law the rights and actions of the nationals of the hostile party'.[16] The generally recognized exceptions to this prohibition permit the occupant to deprive indigenous courts of jurisdiction over soldiers of the occupying power[17] and over civilian agents of the occupant.[18] But it is admitted, even by those who support a contrary view, that such areas of civil law as those governing 'property, debts, most contracts ... commercial activities, and so on' are generally held to be 'immune from interference' by the occupant.[19]

The abolition of major civil causes of action would thus unlawfully produce a system, similar to that of the Capitulations, whereby important rights of the Palestinian inhabitants would be absolutely subject to the extraterritorial privileges of the Jewish settlers. This in itself is a sufficient criticism of such extraterritoriality, aside from the dangers of abuse of their special position by settlers who might feel themselves in some sense above the law.

Furthermore, from a purely practical perspective, extraterritoriality might combine with such limitations on the jurisdiction of Israeli courts as selectively to bar Palestinian recourse even to them. For it is within the power of the Knesset to limit or legislate away the jurisdiction of Israeli courts as the government finds convenient.[20] It is unlikely that Israel would forgo the option of limiting Palestinian access to the Israeli judicial system in sensitive cases.

Finally, the capitulatory effect of extraterritoriality would prevent criminal prosecutions of Jewish settlers in Administrative Council courts. Punishment of settlers' crimes against Palestinians, as in cases of the sort of vigilantism to be discussed in Chapter 3 below, would be left entirely to the Israeli authorities who might for reasons of politics or national solidarity decline to prosecute.

In summary, Jewish extraterritoriality promotes Israel's goal of territorial supremacy by (1) weakening the authority of the Administrative Council, (2) expanding Israeli influence over the affairs of the territories when legal disputes arise between Jews and Arabs, and (3) helping to frustrate Palestinian recourse to law in defence of rights whose violation could follow from the process of establishing that supremacy.

Control of Water Resources

Similar Israeli supremacy is provided for by the May 1979 Plan amendment requiring that Israel 'will be responsible for planning water administration'.[21] This has been interpreted to mean full Israeli control of West Bank and Gaza water resources[22] such as only a territorial sovereign would normally enjoy. Earlier statements by Israeli Minister of Agriculture Sharon (chairman of the Ministerial Settlement Committee of the Israeli Cabinet) may be understood to support this interpretation. In January 1979 he was reported as saying:

> More than a third of Israel's water comes from Judea and Samaria. It is quite inconceivable that the issue of water, which is intended to serve all the sections of the population, should be in the hands of the Arab population. A joint water network must be established in which Israel will have the decisive authority.[23]

Unfortunately for the Israeli argument, however, it is quite conceivable in law that a people on whose territory a natural resource exists should not be deprived of decisive authority over

15

that resource merely because it is important to another state. This follows from the very concept of territorial sovereignty as in general giving the sovereign exclusive authority over everything in its territory. To replace such authority with that of a foreign state is also to replace indigenous territorial sovereignty with the sovereignty of another, as indeed this provision of the Plan would do. But if the provision envisages an arrogation of authority to Israel for which there is no inherent justification, this should not be taken to signify that Israel's legitimate interests are legally unprotected.

In this century, international legal doctrine has developed increased sophistication in the area of water resources regulation. In 1966 the authoritative International Law Association adopted the Helsinki Rules on the Uses of Waters of International Rivers[24] as a comprehensive statement of existing rules of international law on the subject. Its coverage extends not only to international rivers but also to the 'international drainage basin' of each, i.e.,

> a geographical area extending over two or more States determined by the watershed limits of the system of waters, including surface and underground waters, flowing into a common terminus.[25]

Article IV provides that each state in such a basin is 'entitled, within its territory, to a reasonable and equitable share in the beneficial uses' of the basin's waters. Article V lists eleven of the relevant factors to be considered when determining what is 'reasonable and equitable'. Among them are:

> (b) the hydrology of the basin, including in particular the contribution of water by each basin State; ...
> (d) the past utilization of the waters of the basin, including in particular existing utilization;
> (e) the economic and social needs of each basin State; ...
> (g) the comparative costs of alternative means of satisfying the economic and social needs of each basin State; ...
> (i) the avoidance of unnecessary waste in the utilization of waters of the basin;
> (j) the practicability of compensation to one or more of the co-basin States as a means of adjusting conflicts among uses ...[26]

Detailed application of these principles is beyond the scope of the present book. Several general observations are in order, however.

16

The first is that an 'equitable' share does not necessarily mean an equal share.[27] Secondly, on the principle *ex injuria non oritur jus**, Israel cannot enhance its claims by including under past and present utilization post-1967 use of the occupied territories' water resources in connection with activities impermissible under international law, as, for example, the utilization of water by illegal Israeli civilian settlements.[28] Furthermore, after peace has been achieved, the problem of refugee resettlement has been dealt with, and hundreds of thousands of displaced Palestinians have returned to the territories, the 'economic and social needs' of the West Bank and Gaza will likely be far greater than at present,[29] although the dimensions of those needs may not be fully ascertainable now. Equitable apportionment therefore probably cannot be determined until the parameters of the political solution are clear. This would mean that, since any rights to the use of West Bank water that Israel may have as belligerent occupant could only be temporary[30] and would terminate with the end of occupation, reallocation of water resources could properly remain on the agenda for later negotiations between Israel and the succeeding administration of the territories.

In the meantime, however, Israel's entitlement to her pre-1967 share of water draining naturally from the West Bank into Israel is protected by the rule of international law that a state (here, the succeeding administration)

> in spite of its territorial supremacy, is not allowed to alter the natural conditions of its own territory to the disadvantage of the natural conditions of the territory of a neighbouring State ...[31]

Land

The law of belligerent occupation distinguishes two basic categories of real property: state-owned and private.[32] As regards the latter, Article 46 of the Hague Regulations absolutely prohibits confiscation (i.e. seizure without compensation) of any private property, while Article 52 of the Regulations permits implicitly temporary requisition (use with compensation) of private real property solely 'for the needs of the army of occupation'.[33]

---

* That is, the wrong-doer can gain no right as a consequence of his wrong-doing.

17

State-owned real property is protected by Article 55 of the Regulations which provides:

> The occupying State shall be regarded only as administrator and usufructuary of public buildings, real estate, forests, and agricultural estates belonging to the hostile State and situated in the occupied country. It must safeguard the capital of these properties, and administer them in accordance with the rules of usufruct.

This 'usufructuary rule' means that state-owned (or, 'public') land 'may not be appropriated by a belligerent occupant' or sold[34] and that, although the products of the land may be used by the occupant, its substance must be preserved[35] or, as it is sometimes put, the corpus must not be impaired.[36]

As applied in the case under examination here, the law is thus that Israel, as belligerent occupant, may not use the economic assets of the occupied territories as if she were the permanent sovereign possessing unfettered territorial supremacy and hence may neither alienate land nor put it to uses inconsistent with that prohibition.[37] It is in this light that the Plan provisions on land should be examined.

The *Jerusalem Post*[38] reported those provisions as follows:

> Government-owned lands, which are uncultivated, will be used, as required, for security needs, for Jewish settlement and for refugee rehabilitation.

> Land which is not legally registered in private ownership, but is nevertheless privately cultivated, will be used, as required, for security needs only.

> Similarly, land which is legally registered in private ownership but is not cultivated will be used for security if required. In this case, it will be requisitioned, not confiscated. (The difference is that in requisition, possession is taken by the government but ownership remains vested in the individual.)

> Privately owned and cultivated land will not be used, unless unavoidably required for security or road-building purposes.

One notes that considerations of 'security' pervade these provisions and may be used to justify Israeli control of all land, including that which is privately owned and cultivated. The function of 'security' in the Plan as a principle of exception to generally-recognized requirements of international law is examined in Chapter 3 below where it is demonstrated that in Israeli parlance 'security' is a concept of almost unlimited scope. In particular, the Israeli government has in the past emphasized that 'security' is a prime justification for Jewish settlements in the occupied territories. Thus, although the language of the Plan's provisions appears to exclude use of any but uncultivated government-owned land for settlements, the subjection of all land to possible 'security' use represents, in fact, subjection of all land to possible Jewish settlement.

As indicated above, in its administration of public land (uncultivated or otherwise), Israel is constrained by the usufructuary rule to only temporary measures that would maintain the integrity of the corpus. This requirement would be violated by establishment of Jewish settlements on the land. Their permanence would effectively alienate the agricultural land used by them, while construction of settlement buildings would impair the corpus.[39] In devoting public land to Jewish settlement, Israel would thus commit two breaches of its duty under Article 55 of the Hague Regulations.

Insofar as the 'security' use of public land may imply use for military purposes,[40] the same general restriction applies, with the caveat that exceptional military utilization might be permissible during actual hostilities in the event of an urgent need for some immediately indispensable use.[41] In general, however, Israel is entitled to use public land only for the lawful purposes of the occupation[42] and only within the limits that the indigenous economy of the territories can bear.[43] Israel may not use the economic assets of the territories in her preparations for war[44] nor, by extension, to meet her general defence requirements.

At the other end of the Plan's hierarchy of land, the prohibition of confiscation of privately-owned and cultivated land is even more clear cut. The prohibition's limited exception 'for the needs of the army of occupation'[45] has been interpreted quite restrictively and to the benefit of the inhabitants of occupied territory, and may be taken to apply to immediate needs of the occupation forces such as food, clothing, lodging and transport services.[46] 'Needs of the army of occupation' is thus not a catch-all permitting use for general military purposes, still less for 'security' purposes. Such needs obviously cannot in any circumstances include civilian settlements.

It is interesting that the Plan's provision on privately-owned and cultivated land should mention, besides the 'security' exception, an exception for 'road-building purposes'. One might

19

have expected here a general reservation for eminent domain. Such a reservation would be in order insofar as seizure of private real property for a public purpose enhancing the welfare of the indigenous population is permitted a belligerent occupant.[47] There is no reason to suppose that Israel intends to give up any right of eminent domain, and the mention of road-building purposes may therefore be taken not as a limitation of eminent domain but rather as a provision for a use normally outside eminent domain. That is, road-building under eminent domain needs no exceptional mention and a road-building that does need such mention is presumably not covered by eminent domain. What sort of road-building might this be? Observers have noted that Israeli settlements on the West Bank form a grid pattern tending to split up and atomize the Arab areas and thus facilitate Israeli control.[48] The grid is completed by the construction of roads linking the Israeli colonies with each other and with Israel. The planning of such roads is an integral part of the settlement programme itself.[49] Israeli Agriculture Minister Sharon, who is Chairman of the Ministerial Settlement Committee, has gone so far as to say that the 'road network cutting across Judea and Samaria is no less important – it may be more important – than Jordan Valley settlement'.[50] And Jordan Valley settlement Mr Sharon has on other occasions regarded as so important that he has recommended doubling the number of settlements in that area.[51] The road network may therefore be taken as a top priority in the Israeli settlement programme, and it is reasonable to assume that it is for those 'road-building purposes' (clearly not eligible for eminent domain on the grounds of benefitting the indigenous Palestinian population) that the Plan wishes to allow seizure even of privately-owned and cultivated land. It follows, however, from the exclusion of settlements as a justification for land seizure that seizure of land for roads linking those settlements and promoting the same aims as those settlements would also be impermissible.

Turning to the Plan's provision for requisitioning of privately-owned but uncultivated Arab land, one notes first that, whereas seizure of cultivated private land is to occur only if 'unavoidably required', no such limitation is placed on the taking of uncultivated private land. That the Plan thus smooths the path for Israeli take-over of uncultivated private land may be taken as a significant indication of the Planner's intentions, given the ways in which Arab land tends to become 'uncultivated' under Israeli administration.

Land may be considered 'uncultivated' if it falls within the category of 'absentee property'. After the war of June 1967, the Israeli Military Custodian of Absentee Property had on the West Bank under his responsibility 328,789 dunums of land and 10,402 buildings.[52] The Custodian acts by virtue of the Israeli Abandoned Property of Private Individuals Order[53] to 'safe-guard' property 'abandoned' by its legal owner or occupier. 'Abandonment' under the Order occurs when 'the legal owner or occupier ... [leaves] the region ... leaving such property within the region'.[54] From the legal perspective this concept of abandonment seems, at the very least, idiosyncratic. For it makes no mention of that intention to relinquish all rights which is the *sine qua non* for abandonment in law.[55] Without that intention, mere leaving of the premises does not constitute abandonment.[56] The Order's omission of this crucial element may be partially explained by the position of the Custodian within the Israeli governmental structure.

For the Custodian's functions are in fact carried out by a section of the Israel Lands Authority (I.L.A.)[57] under the Ministry of Agriculture,[58] the umbrella department for Israeli settlement activity. The I.L.A. co-ordinates its work with the Jewish National Fund[59] which in turn co-operates with the Settlement Department of the Jewish Agency.[60] Given the I.L.A.'s central role in finding the land for settlements, one may not be surprised that the Order adopts a definition of abandon-ment that makes this task significantly easier, although it does not extinguish all rights of the owner. The resulting conflict of interest in the Custodian's duties is obliquely reflected in Section 13(a) of the Abandoned Property Order which provides in part:

> Property and any right which any person had in that property immediately prior to its vesting in the officer-in-charge shall be restored to such person or any person taking his place, *but subject to any rights acquired over the property by another party as a result of any act of the officer-in-charge* ... [emphasis supplied]

In other words, the owner may have lost his rights to possession and use of his property – without ever having intended to relinquish those rights – because the Custodian has, under a legally binding commitment, given rights in that property to another. The effect is therefore essentially the same as if the military governor had seized the property for Jewish civilian settlement rather than for the needs of the army of occupation, a seizure that would be impermissible under international law. May the Custodian lawfully accomplish what the military governor is forbidden to do?

Both logic and public policy suggest that he may not. For the laws of belligerent occupation do not aim merely to control the actions of particular government officers while leaving others uncontrolled. Rather, those laws operate to protect the inhabitants of an occupied territory through obligatory rules binding on the entire government of an occupying power in all its dealings, through whichever official, with the population of the occupied area. To argue otherwise would be to say that the protections of international law were merely form without substance.

Furthermore, if Israel were permitted effectively to seize the property of those who have not abandoned it but have only left a region of active hostilities during war, every unscrupulous military conqueror would be encouraged to drive out his enemy's civilian population so as to get legal blessing for grabbing their property. The uprooting of innocent civilians – specifically forbidden by Article 49 of the Fourth Geneva Convention – should not be allowed by means of so transparent a device to pay dividends to the wrong-doer.

In Israel after 1948 Arab land also became 'uncultivated' through procedures first laid down in Israel's Emergency Regulations (Cultivation of Waste Lands) Ordinance (1949). The role of these procedures in the seizure of Arab land has been described by Sabri Jiryis:

> The minister of defence, or the military governor, would declare an area closed or a security zone, whereby entry without written permit became a serious security offence. At the same time, for 'security reasons', permits could not be issued to the owners of the land to get to it and farm it. The land soon became 'uncultivated', and was immediately declared 'uncultivated land' by the minister of agriculture. At this point, 'in order to ensure that it is cultivated', he could have such land farmed either by 'laborers in his own employ' or by 'handing it over to someone else to farm'. Invariably, the 'other party' was a neighboring Jewish settlement.[61]

Autonomy for people but not for land would give the Administrative Council no authority to hinder Israeli application of similar methods in the occupied territories if the Israeli authorities choose to invoke the pretext of 'security'. Thus, rather than providing for beneficial utilization of waste lands, the Plan's provisions on uncultivated land may establish a basis for large-scale seizure of the best Arab agricultural land. Seen in this light, the Plan's statement that uncultivated private land would only be requisitioned for 'security' purposes appears the scantiest fig leaf to cover a patent illegality.

One comes finally to the Plan's provision for land 'not legally registered in private ownership' but 'nevertheless' privately cultivated. On its face this language seems aimed at land tilled by squatters who have no legal rights at all in the land, so that confiscation of it, otherwise forbidden by Article 46 of the Hague Regulations even if for 'security' purposes, would hurt no one. In fact, however, the provision clearly covers[62] a category of land holding in which private rights are very much at stake: *miri* land. The point is explained by Raphael Patai in his description of land ownership in the West Bank and Jordan:

> The land from which the village derives its livelihood falls into five legal categories. The most common of these is the so-called *miri* which is owned by the state with the right of usufruct vested in a private owner. The right is as a rule permanent and unlimited and can be sold or passed on in inheritance. To all practical purposes therefore *miri* land belongs to its holder.[63]

In general, therefore, the holder is entitled, even though his *miri* land is 'not legally registered' in his name, to demand from the government that it leave him in quiet possession of his holding and that it not interfere with his usufructuary interest. The Plan would undermine this most common of Arab land tenures by asserting a role for the government that runs counter to generations of legal custom and tradition. Such disruption of *miri* holders' rights would be a clear violation of Israel's duty under international law to respect, unless absolutely prevented, the existing laws in the occupied territories[64] and to introduce no changes inimical to the best interests of the indigenous population.[65]

In general, then, the Plan's land provisions, in the light of their specific legal effects, can be seen to arrogate to the Israeli occupation regime authority far beyond that permitted by international law to a belligerent occupant. Indeed, the Plan's attacks on Palestinian proprietary rights recall the Israeli government's assault on Arab land ownership in Israel after 1948, and one may reasonably conclude that the Plan aims to enable Israel to achieve in the occupied territories similar massive transfers of Palestinian property into Israeli hands once 'autonomy' is instituted.[66]

Furthermore, in Israel the transfer of Arab land, the Palestinians' basic economic resource, to Jewish hands was accompanied by the 'transformation of the Palestinian peasantry into a stratum of marginal proletariat'[67] working at manual and unskilled jobs in Israeli-controlled enterprises and condemned to a 'subordinate position in the power structure of Israeli society'.[68] There is statistical evidence that the pressures of occupation are already producing some movement of the territories' Palestinian workers out of indigenous agriculture and into the Israeli construction and unskilled labour sectors.[69] If the Plan's land provisions are allowed to be implemented, with the consequent augmentation of those pressures, the stage will then be fully set for a replay in the occupied territories of the broad disruption of Palestinian society accomplished earlier in Israel itself.

NOTES

1 The Begin Plan, Art. 9.
2 *See* N.Y.Times, May 22, 1979, p.1, col.1.
3 *See* N.Y. Times, May 18, 1979, p.1, cols. 4 & 5.
4 Begin Plan, Art. 17.
5 *Id.*, Art. 19.
6 *Id.*, Art. 21.
7 As regards existing legislation, the law of belligerent occupation requires in general that the occupant respect 'unless absolutely prevented' the laws in force in the occupied territory at the time of occupation: Hague Regulations, Chapter One, note 20, Article 43. However, as will be discussed in Chapter 3, Israel does not acknowledge that it is legally bound by the entire law of belligerent occupation, at least as regards the West Bank. On the basis of that contention, Israel could argue that it is not legally bound to respect any pre-existing law.
8 Begin Plan, Art. 9.
9 N.Y. Times, May 9, 1979, p.A 11, col. 1.
10 BLACK'S LAW DICTIONARY (4th ed.) *sub voc.* 'EXTRA-TERRITORIALITY'.
11 I LAUTERPACHT-OPPENHEIM 845, and also 49, 50, 682–686.

12 LEWIS, THE EMERGENCE OF MODERN TURKEY (2nd ed., O.U.P. paperback) at 183: '... the Ottoman courts, limited in their competence to cases involving Ottoman subjects only ...'
On arbitration, *see* HOLT, EGYPT AND THE FERTILE CRESCENT 1516–1922 (Cornell paperback) at 197 *and* MARLOWE, A HISTORY OF MODERN EGYPT AND ANGLO-EGYPTIAN RELATIONS (2nd ed.) at 86–87.

13 LANDES, BANKERS AND PASHAS 90 (Harper Torchbook ed. (1969)).

14 This understanding of the Plan's intention is shared by Egypt and the United States, reportedly prompting American proposals that the Council's powers should go beyond those envisaged in the Plan and include judicial authority as well. Boston Globe, Aug. 5, 1979, p.1.

15 Hague Regulations, Chapter One, note 20 *supra*.

16 *See* GERSON, ISRAEL, THE WEST BANK AND INTERNATIONAL LAW 123 for applicability of Article 23 to belligerent occupation, *and also* VON GLAHN, LAW AMONG NATIONS (3rd ed.) at 673, *and* II LAUTERPACHT-OPPENHEIM 445.

17 GERSON, *id*. at 124.

18 VON GLAHN, op cit., at 674.

19 *Id*. 673.

20 For example, proposals were reported that would foreclose recourse to Israeli courts by Israeli Bedouin citizens objecting to seizure by the government of their land in the Negev for construction of Israeli military bases being relocated from the Sinai in consequence of the Egyptian-Israeli Peace Treaty. *See* TIME, August 6, 1979, at 52–53.

21 N.Y. Times, May 9, 1979, p.A 11, col. 1.

22 N.Y. Times, May 15, 1979, p.A 3, cols. 1 & 2.

23 Quoted from *Ma'ariv* in Ekin, 'Water in the Occupied Territories', MERIP REPORTS, No. 78, June 1979, at 14.

24 INTERNATIONAL LAW ASSOCIATION, REPORT OF THE FIFTY-SECOND CONFERENCE 477–533, Chapters 1 & 2 *reprinted* in BROWNLIE PUBLIC 273–275.

25 Helsinki Rules, Article II.

26 Set out in BROWNLIE PUBLIC 274.

27 Cf. Khadduri, Dixon & Anthony, 'Other Territorial and

Jurisdictional Issues', in MAJOR MIDDLE EAST PROBLEMS IN INTERNATIONAL LAW 95, at 109 (ed. Khadduri).

28 Cf. Testimony of Paul Quiring in ISRAELI SETTLE-MENTS IN THE OCCUPIED TERRITORIES, HEARINGS BEFORE THE SUB-COMMITTEES ON INTERNATIONAL ORGANIZATIONS AND ON EUROPE AND THE MIDDLE EAST OF THE COMMITTEE ON INTERNATIONAL RELATIONS HOUSE OF REPRESENTATIVES ... September 12, 21, and October 19, 1977, p.43, at 46–48. (Hereinafter, this source will be cited as HEARINGS.) *Also*, Ekin, note 23 *supra*; *and* LESCH, POLITICAL ASPIRATIONS OF THE PALESTINIANS ON THE WEST BANK AND THE GAZA STRIP, Chapter 6, section on 'The Impact of Israeli Colonies'.

29 For a recent study and projections *see* TUMA & DARIN-DRABKIN, THE ECONOMIC CASE FOR PALESTINE 74–78.

30 Cf. Skubiszewski, 'Use of Force by States. Collective Security. Law of War and Neutrality', in SØRENSEN 739, at 833.

31 I LAUTERPACHT-OPPENHEIM 290.

32 Cf. Skubiszewski, note 30 *supra*, at 833–834; GERSON, note 16 *supra*, at 159–169; VON GLAHN, note 16 *supra*, at 680–683.

Cf. BRITISH MANUAL OF MILITARY LAW, Part III, p.164, Para. 592; VON GLAHN, note 16 *supra*, at 683.

34 VON GLAHN, op. cit., at 680.

35 *Id*.

36 Cf. GERSON, note 16 *supra*, at 161. *See also*, in general, Clagett & Johnson, 'May Israel as a Belligerent Occupant Lawfully Exploit Previously Unexploited Oil Resources of the Gulf of Suez?', 72 A.J.I.L. 558–585, where the question posed in the article's title is answered in the negative.

37 Cf. II LAUTERPACHT-OPPENHEIM (7th ed.) at 397–398 (illegality of appropriation and alienation of public land), 403 (similarly as to private real property) and 618–619 on the effects of postliminium invalidity of acts by an occupant which it, not being sovereign, was incompetent to perform. *Also*, Clagett & Johnson, op. cit., at 584.

38 The Jerusalem Post Int'l Ed., May 20–26, 1979.

39 On the latter point, *see* GERSON, note 16 *supra*, at 161.

40 The N.Y. Times report of May 9, 1979, p.A 11, col. l, in fact reports the phrase 'military purposes' in this provision of the Plan.

41 Cf. Hague Regulations, Article 23(g):
'it is especially forbidden ... to destroy or seize the enemy's property, unless such destruction or seizure be imperatively demanded by the necessities of war.'

42 *See* Clagett & Johnson, note 35 *supra*, at 581.

43 *Id*.

44 *Id*. at 582.

45 Hague Regulations, Art. 52.

46 *See* GERSON, note 16 *supra*, 164; II LAUTERPACHT-OPPENHEIM 409–410.

47 Cf. VON GLAHN, note 16 *supra*, at 683; X WHITEMAN, DIGEST OF INTERNATIONAL LAW 577.

48 LESCH, note 27 *supra*, Chapter 6, section on 'The Impact of Israeli Colonies.'

49 E.g., Jer. Post, Jan. 18, 1979, p.1 reported the Knesset Finance Committee's approval of a settlements budget that included funds for a trans-Samaria road linking new settlements.

50 Jerusalem Post, Dec. 15, 1979, p.2.

51 *See* N.Y. Times, May 31, 1979, p.A9, cols. 1–4.

52 GERSON, note 16 supra, at 189, note 108.

53 Military Order No. 10 of July 23, 1967, discussed in GERSON at 141 with partial English translation at 198, note 180.

54 Abandoned Property of Private Individuals Order, Section 1(a).

55 BLACK'S LAW DICTIONARY (4th ed.) *sub voc.* 'ABANDONMENT.'

56 *Id., sub voc.* 'ABANDONMENT-PROPERTY.'

57 N.Y. Times, April 12, 1976, p.1, col. 6.

58 Cf. ISRAELI GOVERNMENT YEARBOOK 1967/68 at 75, reporting on what is there translated as the Israel Lands Directorate. Other translations sometimes refer to it as the Israel Lands Administration.

59 N.Y. Times, April 12, 1976, p. 1, col. 6.

60 *See* Ministry of Information, Jerusalem, FACTS ABOUT

ISRAEL (1975) at 142.

61 S. JIRYIS, THE ARABS IN ISRAEL 95.

62 Cf. Boston Globe, Oct. 25, 1979, reporting that Israeli government lawyers had produced 'a new legal definition' to facilitate seizure of unregistered land 'tilled for generations by Arab families.'

63 R. PATAI, THE KINGDOM OF JORDAN 202.

64 Hague Regulations, Article 43.

65 GERSON, note 16 *supra*, at 170.

66 Cf. Ruedy, 'Dynamics of Land Alienation', in THE TRANSFORMATION OF PALESTINE 119, at 134–138, indicating: that 72 per cent of land cultivated by Jews in 1949 had been Arab-owned in 1948; that 40 per cent of the real property held by Arab citizens of Israel was confiscated under absentee property regulations which were applied to cover Israeli Arabs who had never left the country but had merely moved temporarily from one part of Israel to another; and that by 1953 the Custodian of absentee property had effectively sold 2, 373, 677 dunums of land for settlement purposes. It has been pointed out that these seizures were a direct violation of the United Nations Partition Plan for Palestine which declared in Chapter 2, Paragraph 8:

    'No expropriation of land owned by an Arab in the Jewish State ... shall be allowed except for public purposes. In all cases of expropriation full compensation as fixed by the Supreme Court shall be paid previous to dispossession.'

    See, E. ZUREIK, THE PALESTINIANS IN ISRAEL 119–120, quoting PERETZ, ISRAEL AND THE PALESTINE ARABS 126.

67 ZUREIK, op. cit., at 131.

68 *Id.* at 200–201.

69 *See* TUMA & DARIN-DRABKIN, note 28 *supra*, p.52, indicating that between 1968 and 1975 although the Palestinian work force employed in the West Bank grew from 84,000 to 92,000, the percentage of workers employed in West Bank agriculture dropped from 39% to 35%. In the same period, employment in Israel of Arabs from the occupied territories of Gaza and the West Bank absorbed 87% of the increase in the total work force of those territories. Thus, by 1975, of the total work force of 205,000

persons, 66,000 worked in Israel, 55% of them in the construction sector and 15% in Israeli agriculture. Comparatively, whereas in 1968 indigenous agriculture absorbed the largest block of these territories' total work force (45,000 out of a total of 135,000, or 33% of the total), in 1975 employment in Israel had become the largest block (32% of the total) while indigenous agriculture came a poor second (44,000 out of 205,000, only 21% of the total).

3   Israel's Territorial Supremacy under the Plan: 'Security and Public Order'

Although Article 10 of the Begin Plan envisaged operation by the Administrative Council of 'the department for ... the supervision of the local police forces', Article 11 reserved a potentially far more significant role for Israel:

> Security and public order ... will be the responsibility of the Israeli authorities.

Assuming even the maximum independence for the Council's police force on the local level, the Plan would be establishing a structure not substantially dissimilar from that prevailing in federal states where local police powers are allotted to subordinate (or independent) authorities while security powers are exercized by the governmental unit that is sovereign on the international level.[1] It follows from the discussion in Chapter 1 on retention of paramount authority by the occupant that the existence in the occupied territories of a legal or police apparatus not wholly controlled by the occupation regime would not be inconsistent with continued belligerent occupation. Indeed, under Article 43 of the Hague Regulations, the belligerent occupant is required to exert its *de facto* authority to ensure 'public order and safety' while 'respecting, unless absolutely prevented', the laws in force in the occupied territories.

Paradoxically, however, it is precisely this Article that raises problems in the interpretation and application of the Plan's provision on 'security and public order'. For, on the one hand, the Regulations in that Article give the occupant responsibility for 'public order' ('*ordre public*' in the French version of the Regulations) and thereby impose on him the duty to protect the indigenous population of the occupied territories by maintaining law and order and checking all violence and crime. On the other hand, the Article also gives the occupant power to act, not out of considerations of security, but from concern for public 'safety' (*vie publique*). This English rendering 'safety' is somewhat unsatisfactory, as *vie publique* is often understood to involve not the protection of the indigenous inhabitants' physical well-being but rather the safeguarding of their general welfare and quality of life.[2] Given the Begin Plan's conferring on the Administrative Council responsibility for housing, health, labour and social welfare,[3] 'security' under the Plan does not appear intended to be equivalent to 'safety' under the Regulations. What, then, does 'security' mean, and why was it substituted for 'safety'? What are the effects of that substitution?

'Security' as a Principle of Exception

If the rubric 'security and public order' is foreign to Article 43, the general 'purpose provision'[4] of the Hague Regulations, and to a corresponding provision in the Fourth Geneva Convention,[5] whence does it come?

The answer may lie in two important international charters of human rights. The United Nations International Covenant on Civil and Political Rights[6] provides in Article 12(3) that certain enumerated rights of free movement may be subject to restrictions 'necessary to protect national security' and 'public order'. Public trials may be restricted under Article 14(1) for reasons of 'public order... or national security in a democratic society'. Thus, in the Covenant security and public order may serve in specific and narrow instances as justification for partial limitation on the Covenant's broad fundamental rights which, by implication, are otherwise to be respected by democratic governments in dealings with their own citizens.

A recent treatise on international law, in a sub-section headed 'Security and public order',[7] points out that the European Convention on Human Rights[8] similarly permits some limited restrictions on its enumerated rights when 'public emergency' or the 'interests of national security' warrant. Yet, even under Article 15(1) of the Convention, a state's right of derogation in time of 'war or public emergency threatening the life of the nation' extends only to measures

strictly required by the exigencies of the situation, provided that such measures are not inconsistent with its other obligations under international law.

Article 15(2) prohibits derogation even in an emergency from the right to life or from the right not to be subject to torture or inhuman or degrading treatment or punishment. Beyond thus subjecting the state's power of derogation to fundamental rights and to the requirements of international law, the Convention also empowers the European Commission and the European Court of Human Rights to 'ensure'[9] the signatory states' adherence to the Convention by examining, when called upon, attempts to invoke rights of derogation.

It may well be, then, that the Begin Plan's use of the phrase 'security and public order' was modelled on these charters as a means of introducing into the operation of the Israeli military government during autonomy an element of sovereign-like discretionary power not found in the Hague Regulations and the Fourth Geneva Convention. But, while in the human rights charters such power is hedged about and restricted to exceptional situations, the Begin Plan would appear to confer on the occupation regime all the power without any of the limitations. Under the Plan, the exception becomes the rule as Israel is left solely responsible for determining what constitutes 'security' and what measures it may justify.

Israel's Concept of Security

The breadth that the Israeli government is prepared publicly to attach in a court of law to the concept of 'security' was manifest in a significant case before the Israeli High Court of Justice in 1978. Non-public or extra-legal Israeli definitions of 'security' may reasonably be assumed to be even broader.

Sliman Tawfik Ayoub et al v. *the Minister of Defence* (hereinafter to be referred to as the *Beit El* case after the site involved) was brought in the High Court of Justice by Palestinian owners of land on the West Bank who requested a permanent injunction to forbid the Israeli military authorities from maintaining and expanding an Israeli civilian settlement on the plaintiffs' land that previously had been 'seized' for 'military requirements' by order of the Israeli area commander.[10] In answer to the plaintiffs' contentions that, under the Hague Regulations and the Fourth Geneva Convention, the defendants could only temporarily requisition private property for the needs of the army of occupation and could not in any case permit the land to be used for purposes of civilian settlement, the government presented a defence based almost entirely on its concept of security. The argument in the Government Affidavit was framed in this way:

15. According to the rules of international law it is permitted to seize private property for military requirements... The military requirement for the seizure of this area... still exists... This military requirement precludes any use whatsoever by the petitioners of the real estate concerned... in these circumstances the respondents may make any use of the real estate being the subject of the petition that does not conflict with the military requirement...

16(a). Moreover... establishment of the settlement in the area of the Beit El [army] camp not only does not conflict with the military requirement but actually serves it, in that it is a part of the security conception of the Government which bases security *inter alia* on Jewish settlements. In accordance with this concept all Israeli settlements in the territories occupied by the I[srael] D[efence] F[orces] constitute part of the I.D.F.'s regional defence system... In times of calm these settlements serve mainly for the purpose of presence and control of vital areas, for maintaining observation, and the like. The importance of these settlements is enhanced in particular in time of war when the regular army forces are shifted, in the main, from their bases for purposes of operational activation and the said settlements constitute the principal component of presence and security control in the areas in which they are located.

(b). The [army] camp at Beit El is situated on a site of major importance from a security aspect...
The settlement itself is located on a lofty site that controls a vital road junction of major importance... In addition, the site where the settlement has been established controls infrastructure systems (water, electricity, communications) that are of importance in regard to wide areas... Moreover... it is the defence establishment's intention to put up a system of fortifications in the settlement.

34

Several observations may be offered on the concept of security revealed in these arguments. Firstly, it is clear that security is not merely a matter of response to imminent danger but, on the contrary, extends easily to long-term issues such as 'the I.D.F.'s regional defence system', and to strategic topography, systems of fortifications, and even economic infrastructure. Security encompasses mere Israeli civilian presence in the occupied territories and could thereby conceivably be extended to the demographics of that presence. Indeed, the concept is so far-reaching that it is capable of being taken in some circumstances to permit anything 'that does not conflict with the military requirement'.

Is such an expansive notion of 'security' reconcilable with the law of belligerent occupation?

'Military Necessity' and the Law of Belligerent Occupation

The 'military necessity' which may justify specific exceptional departures from the laws of war and belligerent occupation has been distinguished from the right of states to employ force in 'self-defence'. While self-defence against armed attack may in current international law justify the strategic decision to embark on war, '[m]ilitary necessity should be confined to the plight in which armed forces may find themselves under stress of active warfare'.[11] In this context, military necessity has been defined as 'an urgent need, admitting of no delay',[12] or as a need for something 'immediately indispensable' to a 'legitimate military end'.[13] Thus, when the heat of battle has passed, the need is no longer urgent, delay is admissible, or when alternative legitimate means are available for achieving a legitimate military (as opposed to political) end, then no military necessity could properly be claimed.

To argue otherwise is to expand what are narrow exceptions to the humanitarian provisions of the laws of war into general rules standing in opposition to those laws. In the late nineteenth century, German theorists attempted just this in proposing that military necessity (*Kriegsraison*) in certain circumstances justified actions in excess of the laws of war, thereby, in the words of one scholar, reducing 'the entire body of the laws of war to a code of military convenience, having no further sanction than the sense of honour of the individual military commander or chief of staff...'[14] But, in fact, the Hague Regulations clearly state that the right to adopt means of injuring the enemy is not unlimited.[15] Further- more, '[c]ourts have had occasion to reject emphatically the view that the ensuring of the success of the war justifies recourse to the doctrine of military necessity'.[16] While the laws of war may permit limited exceptions to their general rules, such exceptions could not in logic deny those laws' own underlying and formative humanitarian principles. Indeed, military necessity was already discounted from the Hague Regulations when they were written so that the rules therein are not subject to exceptions for military necessity unless that is specifically stated.[17] Hence military necessity never provides legitimate justification for illegal acts in contravention of the laws of war. Thus, the concept of military necessity

> authorizes the use of all of the means to which... [the belligerent]... is *entitled*. If these are still not enough, then legally there is no alternative to defeat.[18] [emphasis supplied]

With this rigorous standard imposed even during actual hostilities, when the fate of a nation may hang in the balance from moment to moment, it is clear that no less rigorous a standard could be justified during belligerent occupation when, by definition, the occupant, far from facing imminent disaster, has in fact so far overcome its enemy as actually to have established the occupant's authority over the enemy's territory.[19]

It should be noted that belligerent occupation (and hence the law of belligerent occupation with its duties imposed on the occupant) 'does not become invalid because some of the inhabitants are in a state of rebellion, or through occasional successes of guerrilla bands or "resistance" fighters'.[20]

Set against international law's restricted concept of 'military necessity', the Israeli notion of 'security' seems in many ways more attuned to *Kriegsraison*'s 'code of military convenience'. This is particularly evident in the Israeli application of 'security' to the question of the Beit El settlement. The argument quoted at length above quite clearly indicates that the settlement's role is to perform, not merely during active warfare but even in 'times of calm', military functions which, implicitly, the army finds not impossible but merely inconvenient to perform. Yet even the impossibility of the army's performing those functions would not confer the requisite necessity on civilian settlements in view of failure to meet the test of 'an urgent need' for some 'immediately indispensable' act. Furthermore, if the particular act (e.g. settlement) for which Israel seeks justification does not benefit from a specific exception when in general such acts are proscribed by the laws of war (as with transfer of civilian population for any purpose, including settlement), then even if the act is militarily indispensable and urgently needed, Israel still may not lawfully carry it out. To this extent at least, it may fairly be said that what the law of war does not specifically permit, it forbids. Thus, in this context, the Israeli argument that 'security' may justify anything that 'does not conflict with the military requirement' fails.

Although 'security' thus cannot excuse even some of the quasi-military activities to which Israel would like it applied, the Israeli government persists in seeking yet wider scope for the concept in its belligerent occupation.

The Bir Zeit Situation

The 1979 closure for security reasons of Bir Zeit University, a Palestinian institution of higher learning on the West Bank, provides an illuminating example of the expansion of 'security' into a concept of political control. As reported in the *New York Times*,[21] a high Israeli official, when asked for hard evidence of Bir Zeit involvement in such activities as terrorism, replied:

> Look, we have no positive proof that Bir Zeit is an Al Fatah cell... If we did we'd break up the cell. But we have caught lots of students of Bir Zeit who were mixed up in subversive activities. Talk to any Bir Zeit student and he is against Israel...
> The West Bank is occupied territory, and the military government can, for security reasons, take any measures it considers necessary.

The reasoning here is apparently as follows: to be a Palestinian in occupied territory who is against Israel is to be subversive; to be subversive is to endanger 'security'; and, military occupation gives *carte blanche* for 'any measures' in the name of security.

One may infer from this that the Israeli authorities would

claim, as part of their entitlement to take 'any measures', the prerogative of infringing political, and, if need be, individual, rights. Some confirmation of this inference was given in the same *Times* report by Major-General Chaim Herzog, former West Bank military governor and Israeli ambassador to the United Nations. He was quoted as putting the problem faced by the Israeli authorities in this way:

> whether a body [like Bir Zeit University] is allowed to hide behind the concept of freedom of speech in order to try to destroy the country in which it exists.

The perhaps unwitting juxtaposition of limitations on Palestinian rights of free speech with Herzog's implicit inclusion of the West Bank in Israel indeed adds a significant dimension to the Israeli notion of 'security'. The role of the occupier is no longer to use its authority to protect the physical safety of its troops and preserve law and order for the indigenous inhabitants, but also to use its power to impose on the occupied territory the occupier's vision of ultimate political realities. Opposition to that vision becomes a matter of 'security' which the occupier may protect by 'any measures it considers necessary'.

'Security' becomes in the end a catch-all expression encompassing anything that contradicts Israel's intention to exercise territorial supremacy over the occupied territories. As such, it takes its place as the overarching concept that subsumes and is reinforced by what one of the May 1979 amendments called 'the struggle against terror, subversion, and violence' that will 'remain in the hands of the Israeli security services'.[22]

This overarching concept of 'security' makes the Plan in principle incompatible with the spirit and the letter of the relevant international law.

Human Rights under the Law of Belligerent Occupation

This incompatibility is most evident when one considers the purpose and spirit of the Fourth Geneva Convention. These have been well-expressed in the authoritative Commentary on the Convention published by the International Committee of the Red Cross whose preliminary work formed the basis of the four Geneva Conventions of 1949. The Commentary notes that the powers which the Occupying Power is recognized to have are very extensive and complex, but these varied measures must not under any circumstances serve as a means of oppressing the population.[23]

The Commentary's conclusion is supported by Article 47 of the Fourth Convention which, under the heading 'Inviolability of Rights', provides:

Protected persons* who are in occupied territory shall not be deprived, in any case or in any manner whatsoever, of the benefits of the present Convention by any change introduced, as the result of the occupation of a territory, into the institutions or government of the said territory, nor by any agreement concluded between the authorities of the occupied territories and the Occupying Power, nor by any annexation by the latter of the whole or part of the occupied territory.

In other words, the occupant is forbidden to deny protected persons their benefits under the Convention on the excuse that a change of legal status has been effected whereby the areas concerned, though still under the occupant's power, are in some way supposedly withdrawn from the category of occupied territories to which the Convention applies. Agreement of local authorities cannot accomplish such a change because in general they do not represent the whole of the people whose sovereignty over the territory is at stake. Annexation is similarly ineffective because it is a unilateral attempt to interfere with the legal rights of other parties. *A fortiori*, plans for such changes in the future provide even less justification for denial of benefits.

Implicit in Article 47 is the assumption that, except for legally effective change in the status of the occupied territories (as by liberation or through a peace treaty with the legitimate sovereign), they remain occupied and hence fully subject to the law of belligerent occupation. Thus, if the occupant is forbidden to deny protected persons their rights even because of major changes in the territories, so much the less could minor manipulations within the context of occupation provide him an excuse to do so.

---

* 'Persons protected by the Convention are those who, at a given moment and in any manner whatsoever, find themselves, in case of a conflict or occupation, in the hands of a Party to the conflict or Occupying Power of which they are not nationals.' Fourth Convention, Article 4.

It is to be noted that Article 47 speaks not merely of 'rights' but of 'benefits'. This broader language may be taken to include benefits to protected persons consequent on the exercise by others of rights given to them under the Convention. This would cover, for example, the rights conferred on international humanitarian and relief organizations to carry out their varied work on behalf of protected persons according to Articles 10, 30 and 142 of the Convention. That the occupant, under Article 47, may not deny protected persons these benefits is, as will be seen, of considerable significance in the situation of the West Bank and the Gaza Strip.

Turning to the content of the specific rights secured to protected persons under the Convention, one finds that there are two basic categories: rights that are absolute and those that may to some extent be subject to exceptions.

Absolutely prohibited in all circumstances are:
— individual or mass forcible transfers, or deportation of protected persons outside the bounds of the occupied territory (Article 49);
— transfers by the occupant of parts of its own civilian population into the occupied territory (Article 49);
— murder, torture, corporal punishments, mutilation and medical or scientific experiments against protected persons, infliction of physical suffering, or 'any other measures of brutality whether applied by civilian or military agents' (Article 32);
— collective punishment, reprisals against protected persons or their property, and 'all measures of intimidation or of terrorism' (Article 33);
— unlawful confinement of protected persons, and wilfully depriving them of the rights of fair and regular trial (Article 147);
— physical or moral coercion against protected persons for any reason whatever (Article 31);
— all acts of violence or threats thereof, whether committed by agents of the occupation regime or by civilians of the occupying nation (Article 27).

Prohibitions subject to exceptions are:
— prohibition of destruction by the Occupying Power of real or personal property belonging individually or collectively to private protected persons 'except where such destruction is rendered absolutely necessary by military operations' (Article 53);

40

— prohibition of adverse distinctions in treatment of protected persons 'based, in particular, on race, religion or political opinion', subject, however, to 'such measures of control and security in regard to protected persons as may be necessary as a result of the war' (Article 27), it being understood, in the words of the I.C.R.C. Commentary, that those measures 'should not affect the fundamental rights of the persons concerned... those rights must be respected even when measures of constraint are justified'.[24]

This enumeration indicates that the most fundamental and significant rights of protected persons are in the category of rights that are subject to no exceptions or derogations. Their vindication may therefore be legitimately claimed on all appropriate occasions regardless of the effect this might have on the occupier's policies or programmes.

In this light it is not difficult to see why Israel's entitlement under international law to exercise, within the framework of those absolute rights, the authority under the Hague Regulations to secure 'public order and safety' has been found by the drafters of the autonomy Plan to be insufficient for their purposes. For, assuming that Israeli human rights violations are in general neither gratuitous nor superfluous but are rather motivated by a clear conception of Israeli self-interest, one may reasonably infer that disregard of Palestinian rights has been, and continues to be, viewed by the Israeli authorities as necessary to the success of their policies. The Plan has confirmed that a principal element in those policies is Israeli territorial supremacy in the occupied territories and it may well be thought that human rights violations are part of the process by which that supremacy is to be achieved.

The Bir Zeit case discussed above demonstrated the identity in Israeli thinking between independent Palestinian political activity and 'security' offences. The military governor of the West Bank, Brigadier Ben-Eliezer, later evinced the same outlook in an interview. After emphasizing that he was unyielding in the 'security' field, he went on to say that the Palestinians of the area

> understand that there's a limit which can't be passed... They know that the game goes just this far... and no further.[25]

Asked then whether Israel would permit Palestinian political activity on the West Bank, the Brigadier replied:

I'm not against their legitimate right to stand up and say what they feel. But I am against political activity which wants to say 'no' to the peace process and 'no' to autonomy...[26]

He concluded:

The Arabs of Judea and Samaria have to understand... that they can live alongside us, love us, learn our customs and behaviour...[27]

All this may reasonably be understood to mean that the limit beyond which the military governor feels justified in using his 'security' powers permits no political disagreement with the Israeli version of autonomy even though that might seriously undermine Palestinian rights in international law. Indeed 'security' could conceivably reach to Palestinian failure to 'love' Israel or Palestinian resistance to learning Israeli 'customs and behaviour'. In short, Israel's political goals are being protected through military government 'security' powers that far exceed what is permitted under the laws of belligerent occupation but that probably could not be restricted without damaging consequences for Israel's political ambitions. The present manifestations of this situation may therefore be examined as guides to the likely effect of incorporating into the autonomy arrangements Israel's concept of 'security'.

Israeli Human Rights Violations

1   *Deportations*

Although Article 49 of the Fourth Geneva Convention absolutely forbids deportation of protected persons outside the occupied territories (even to the unoccupied portions of their own state), the Israeli authorities have deported for 'security reasons' over 1150 individuals since the war of June 1967.[28] International law confers no legality even on deportation of West Bankers with Jordanian passports to Jordan, let alone deportation of non-Jordanian Gazans to Jordan or of West Bankers to Lebanon. Indeed, the law is clear on the point that deportation is not merely an illegality but a war crime,[29] and yet the Israeli autonomy Plan would strengthen Israel's ability to continue the practice without restraint.

42

This book is not the place for a detailed examination of the many charges – some even supported by lie detector evidence[30] – of torture inflicted on Palestinian political prisoners detained by the Israeli security services. It is important, however, to consider the conceptual weakness in such examinations of the problem as the U.S. State Department's annual human rights reports.

In its 1978 report the State Department acknowledged that there were 'instances of brutality' in Israeli treatment of Palestinian prisoners, but concluded that it had no evidence 'that Israel follows a consistent practice or policy of using torture'.[31] The 1979 report noted that allegations continued of 'systematic' torture and acknowledged once again that the 'accumulation of reports... make it appear that instances of mistreatment have occurred'.[32]

Close scrutiny of the Fourth Geneva Convention's relevant provisions enumerated above suggests that this concern with whether torture is 'systematic' may be misplaced. For although Article 32 (in prohibiting parties to the Convention from 'taking any measures of such a character as to cause' torture) may be taken to apply to 'systematic' torture, the language of Article 27 imposes a duty on the belligerent occupant positively to protect the inhabitants of the territories 'especially against all acts of violence or threats thereof'. As stated by the I.C.R.C. Commentary:

> The Convention does not confine itself to stipulating that such acts are not to be committed. It goes further: it requires States to take all precautions and measures in their power to prevent such acts and assist the victims in case of need.[33]

Thus, even if responsible Israeli authorities have not in fact decided on the use of torture as a policy, the Israeli government may still be liable for failing to prevent torture. It is not necessary, then, to establish that torture is 'systematic' in order to make the case that the Israeli occupation regime is in breach of international law on this point.

The Israeli response to torture charges is that torture is not official Israeli policy and that all allegations of its use are investigated.[34] This begs the question, however. The real issue, in the light of Article 27 of the Convention, is that, after thirteen years of occupation in which to deal with the problem of torture, Israel, with what is said to be one of the world's most efficient security services, has proved incapable of stamping out the practice of torture by its own agents.

In this connection, an observation of the European Court of Human Rights in its 1978 judgement in *Ireland* v. *The United Kingdom* appears apposite. Considering charges of ill-treatment of detainees, the Court declared that

> the higher authorities of a State... are strictly liable for the conduct of their subordinates; they are under a duty to impose their will on subordinates and cannot shelter behind their inability to ensure that it is respected.[35]

On this basis the evident incapacity of the Israeli Government to impose on its subordinate security officials what it claims to be its will would not absolve it from liability.

Furthermore, there is also a question of whether such long-term incapacity is not itself in some sense 'systematic'.

In sum, given the positive duty on the occupying power to prevent violence to protected persons, Israel's failure is a breach of the Convention. An autonomy arrangement that would allow this violation to continue would in turn be contrary to international law.

For the persistent evidence of such an incapacity (resulting either from policy or from failure of policy) allows the reasonable conclusion that what the Israeli authorities could not eradicate in thirteen years of occupation they will not eliminate in the five years proposed for autonomy. Therefore, to accept the security provisions of the Plan would be to accept that Palestinians will continue, on whatever scale, to suffer torture at the hands of the Israeli security services.

3 Civilian vigilantism and military brutality

Coinciding with the initiation of Egyptian-Israeli talks on Palestinian autonomy, there occurred an upsurge in the occupied territories of Jewish settler vigilante activity against the indigenous Palestinian population. Many incidents of this Jewish vigilantism were documented and commented upon in both the Israeli and foreign press.[36] On June 1, 1979, the *Washington Post* reported in part as follows:

Abdul Aziz, a 42 year-old part-time messenger in [Hebron] city hall, was watching television [on] Saturday night with his wife and four children in their tiny stone house in Hebron's casbah when they heard a frightful pounding on their door. Four armed men burst inside, shouting in Hebrew and waving their weapons.

'Why are you living here?' one demanded, shifting to Arabic, while the others, dressed in civilian clothes and wearing skull-caps, began wrecking the living room.

One cracked the front of the television set with his boot, while others smashed a glass coffee table, broke a chair and threw glasses of hot tea on the floor.

'You are living in a Jewish house. Get out!' one tall Hebrew-speaking man shouted at Aziz, who tried to explain that his father and grandfather had lived in the house. The men began beating Aziz as his children cried hysterically and his wife ran screaming outside...

Before the night was over, three houses in the casbah had been similarly terrorized, city officials said. Several more on the outskirts of town were reportedly stoned by the roaming gang.

At a nearby clinic owned by Dr. Hammad Fawzi Karaki, a nurse, Hadra Ahmed Hassani, said she was tending to patients in midmorning when a gang of armed men, most wearing yarmulkes, burst in. They began tearing pictures off the wall and shouting in English, 'This is our house. Leave,' she said.

A week earlier, a pharmacy next door was broken into by men who claimed the building was Jewish-owned before the massacre of 1929...

On the outskirts of town, vandals with a power saw recently destroyed 500 grape vines tended by an Arab farmer. About 35 miles north, near Ramallah, armed civilians, enraged by the stoning of a schoolbus, opened fire over the heads of demonstrating Arabs. They then burst into an Arab secondary school and abducted its principal, taking him to a settlement for 'questioning' before releasing him to Israeli military authorities.

Still farther north, in the hamlet of Bir Zeit, armed civilians from Neve Tzuf settlement confiscated the identity cards of merchants and forced them to close their shops because Israeli soldiers were pelted by rocks. Almost daily, armed patrols still drive through the hamlet.

In March, two high school students were shot to death in the Arab village of Halhul when civilian settlers opened fire on rock-throwing protesters. Last month, during demonstrations at Bir Zeit University, a student was shot when Jewish settlers opened fire 'in the air' to disperse them.

One settler, who admitted shooting to disperse the crowd, later said he had been issued new ammunition by the army because he had emptied his weapon's magazine. No one has been arrested in the incident, except 14 Arab students who were jailed for three months for demonstrating.

Eliakim Haetzni, a leader of the Council of Jewish Settlements, has issued an appeal in the Ultranationalist Land of Israel Movement's magazine for vigilante recruits. He wrote, 'What will happen if the government of Israel... withdraws... taking with it Israeli law, judges and policemen, leaving us alone to face an emerging Palestinian government?'

'The betrayed and the abandoned,' Haetzni said, would have to provide their own law judges and policemen.

Haetzni says the civilian force will guard the settlements, patrol the surrounding area and enter Arab towns during political meetings and demonstrations...

Even moderate voices in Kiryat Arba [the Jewish settlement from which the Hebron vigilantes were believed to have come], while criticizing such tactics as Saturday night's raids on Arab homes, say that rising tensions in the West Bank call for a certain amount of force.[37]

It is against this background of wide-spread and persistent violence by Jews against Palestinians and of public declarations by vigilante leaders about their intentions that the respect of the Israeli authorities for the obligations imposed on them by international law must be evaluated. The duty of the occupying power under the Fourth Geneva Convention's Article 27 to ensure that protected persons 'shall be protected especially against all acts of violence or threats thereof and against insults' is not lessened merely because terroristic acts of vigilantism are committed by civilian citizens of the occupying power. The Fourth Convention Commentary by the International Committee of the Red Cross indicates that the occupying power is responsible for illegal acts of its citizens in occupied territory

if it has failed to give proof of the requisite diligence and attention in preventing the act contrary to the Convention and in tracking down, arresting and trying the guilty party.[38]

It is clear from the evidence adduced above that the Israeli authorities on numerous occasions failed to prevent vigilante violence even though the provenance of the vigilantes and their intentions were often public knowledge. In the light of these repeated failures a prima facie case exists that Israel has not given 'proof of the requisite diligence and attention' in preventing Jewish violence against Palestinians protected by international law.

Furthermore, there are indications that those failures of the Israeli government encourage illegality to feed upon itself. Thus, for example, Eliakim (or, Elyakim) Haetzni, quoted above as a major proponent of Jewish vigilantism to protect Israeli settlements in occupied territory, also advocates on behalf of the Gush Emunim group seizure of 50,000 acres of Arab land for the expansion of Jewish settlement.[39] In that context, increased vigilante activity appears a means of repressing Arab opposition to the increased illegal settlement that Gush Emunim hopes to promote. Jewish settlement then becomes the *raison d'*être of Jewish violence.

Indeed, one cannot help but consider whether this propensity to violence on the part of Jewish expansionists merely reflects a more general unconcern, in the expansionist circles of the Israeli establishment, with Jewish brutality to Arabs. Several incidents tend to suggest that it may.

For example, in early 1978, in response to a political demonstration by Palestinian school children in Beit Jala, an Arab town on the West Bank not far from Bethlehem, Israeli soldiers forced the students back into their school, closed its windows and doors, and then detonated tear gas bombs inside the building. Some students were injured while jumping from upper windows of the school to escape the noxious effects of the gas in such confined quarters. The West Bank military command attempted a cover-up in the face of press reports of the incident. In May 1978, the West Bank military governor, Brigadier David Hagoel (a graduate of the Hebrew University Law School), was dismissed for failing to investigate the cover-up reports prepared by his subordinates. This dismissal was generally interpreted at the time as an indication that the Israeli government was going to deal rigorously with those responsible in cases of military brutality. In February 1979, however, the *Jerusalem Post* reported that the Minister of Energy intended to appoint Brigadier Hagoel to the key post of Director-General of the Ministry of Energy and Infrastructure.[40]

In mid-1979, controversy raged over decisions by the Israeli Chief of Staff, General Raphael Eitan, to reduce significantly two prison sentences passed by military courts on Israeli service personnel found guilty of murdering Arabs in two separate cases.[41] Former Foreign Minister Abba Eban declared:

when you add these two incidents together, it gives the impression that killing Arabs isn't such a bad thing to do.[42]

Eban was also critical of the effort by military censors to stifle, on the grounds of 'security', press reporting on one of the cases:

It's bad enough that such a thing should happen... To attempt to hush it up merely compounds the crime.[43]

Interestingly, General Eitan, whose leniency towards the convicted murderers provoked Eban's criticism, is known for his open support of the Gush Emunim settlement movement.[44]

In August 1979, the Officer Commanding Israel's Northern Command, Brigadier Avigdor Ben-Gal, was reported to have declared in a speech that Israel's Arab citizens in Galilee were a 'cancer in Israel'.[45] In a statement issued later by the army spokesman, Brigadier Ben-Gal was said to be unable to remember making this remark although he reiterated his concern that the government was neglecting Galilee.[46] This seems to mean that the government was not sufficiently counteracting a growing consciousness and political interest on the part of Galilee Arabs. This appears to be the context in which Brigadier Ben-Gal explained himself by saying 'I compared the neglect of Galilee... to the neglect of a disease'.[47]

Without going further, one may reasonably suspect from these incidents that the men who are responsible for Israel's use of its 'security' power, and who would make the decisions on such use during operation of the Plan's autonomy scheme, are not motivated by any strong impulse to ensure the protection of Palestinians or the maintenance of Palestinian rights in the face of Jewish demands. Some of those men may indeed even be inclined to use their 'security' powers to promote political objectives (such as Jewish settlement) that are directly inimical to Palestinian rights in general and that, as we have seen, may lead to physical violence against Palestinians. In short, those men have not proven themselves by their actions or attitudes to be persons in whom an autonomy arrangement claiming even a semblance of respect for international law could repose any justifiable confidence that they would not misuse their 'security' powers to the detriment of Palestinian rights and even Palestinian lives. Violence and brutality against Palestinians under the Plan's security arrangements are unlikely to abate.

4   *Collective punishment and house demolitions*

The Fourth Geneva Convention's absolute prohibition of collective punishment is contained in Article 33 which in its entirety reads:

ARTICLE 33. — INDIVIDUAL RESPONSIBILITY — COLLECTIVE PENALTIES — PILLAGE — REPRISALS

No protected person may be punished for an offence he or she has not personally committed. Collective penalties and likewise all measures of intimidation or of terrorism are prohibited.

Pillage is prohibited.

Reprisals against protected persons and their property are prohibited.

According to the I.C.R.C. Commentary, the article's prohibition of collective penalties refers to

penalties of any kind inflicted on persons or entire groups of persons, in defiance of the most elementary principles of humanity, for acts these persons have not committed.[48]

The Commentary goes on to make this significant observation:

During past conflicts, the infliction of collective penalties has been intended to forestall breaches of the law rather than to repress them; in resorting to intimidatory measures to terrorise the population, the belligerents hoped to prevent hostile acts. Far from achieving the desired effect, however, such practices, by reason of their excessive severity and cruelty, kept alive and strengthened the spirit of resistance. They strike at guilty and innocent alike. They are opposed to all principles based on humanity and justice and it is for that reason that the prohibition of collective penalties is followed formally by the prohibition of all measures of intimidation or terrorism with regard to protected persons, whatever they may be.[49]

As to reprisals, the Commentary declares:

The prohibition of reprisals is a safeguard for all protected persons... [and] is absolute and mandatory in character and thus cannot be interpreted as containing tacit reservations with regard to military necessity.

...To infringe this provision with the idea of restoring law and order would only add one more violation to those with which the enemy is reproached.

...This paragraph, like the first one, marks a decisive step forward in the affirmation and defence of rights of individuals and there is no longer any question of such rights being withdrawn or attenuated as a result of a breach for which those individuals bear no responsibility. Finally, reprisals constituted a collective penalty bearing on those who least deserved it. Henceforth, the penalty is made individual and only the person who commits the offence may be punished.[50]

It is within this legal framework that relevant Israeli practices in the occupied territories must be considered.

Almost from the beginning of the Israeli occupation in 1967, the military government, with the full approval of then Defence Minister Moshe Dayan, adopted the policy of demolishing houses as, in the words of a leading Israeli journalist, Shabtai Teveth, 'a harsh policy of deterrent and punishment'.[51] General Dayan was said to believe that blowing up houses was 'the most efficient deterrent against collaboration with the terrorist organizations'.[52] Demolitions were carried out in every area of the West Bank, including East Jerusalem.[53] Teveth reports that 'Dayan adhered strictly to the execution of his policy and tried to avoid any compromise out of consideration for people and circumstances'.[54]

Once a person suspected of involvement in anti-Israeli guerrilla activity had been taken into custody, the 'custom was not to delay the demolition but to carry it out as soon after discovery of the act of sabotage as possible'.[55] This meant, of course, that a house with which a suspect was believed to have some association would be demolished long before the suspect was tried and convicted of any crime, a procedure that raises interesting questions about Israeli notions of due process.

To be demolished a house had only to have some association with a suspect and did not need to be the suspect's property. If a suspect rented an apartment from a landlord with whom the suspect was otherwise totally unconnected, the landlord's whole building might be subject to demolition. If a suspect lived with relatives or friends, their house might be destroyed upon his arrest.

The attitude of Israeli commanders who carry out such demolitions is illustrated in the following report by Teveth on a meeting between citizens of the West Bank town of Nablus and one of its early military governors, Lt Col Zvi Ofer, after a series of demolitions which Ofer had personally supervised.[56]

It appeared that two of the demolished houses had belonged to people involved with the saboteurs, but the third had belonged to [the] father of a terrorist...

...one of the participants plucked up enough courage to ask why a father's house should be demolished for the deeds of the son...

'That's a security matter and has nothing to do with you,' calmly returned Ofer, using the stock reply of both himself and Dayan.[57]

Demolition of houses has continued intermittently throughout the period of the occupation, with a notable recrudescence in the period following Palestinian rejection of the Camp David agreements. In January 1979 four West Bank homes were destroyed in one day. The *Jerusalem Post* reported on that incident as follows:

The acts [of demolition] were all reprisals for terror attacks carried out by members of the families owning the houses.

In Abu Dis, on the eastern fringe of Jerusalem, the house belonging to the family of Muhammad Abu Hilal, 24, was demolished. Hilal was apprehended recently and is alleged to have carried out a series of terror acts in the Jerusalem area...

The destroyed house belongs to his uncle. Three families... lived in it.

In Balata, the sprawling refugee camp east of Nablus, the house of Issa Shahshir was demolished...

When the house was destroyed, the mother of the family suffered a nervous collapse and was taken to hospital.

The same procedure was followed by the security forces in all four demolitions. Soldiers arrived on the scene before dawn and proclaimed a curfew. Dwellers in the houses were given more than an hour to remove household effects. In Abu Dis members of the Abu Hilal family responded with shouts and cries, and military government officials removed them from the scene.[58]

Shortly after these demolitions, an interview with Gen. Avraham Orly, retiring Minister of Defence co-ordinator of operations in the occupied territories, appeared in the *Jerusalem Post*. Gen. Orly extolled the Israeli security services for their success in combating terrorism and noted that the lessons of the past had taught the Israeli authorities that 'You need a certain sophistication when you're dealing with one-and-a-half million people'.[59] When asked whether blowing up the houses of terrorist suspects was sophisticated, Orly replied that that was an important component of the overall policy that had led to what-

51

ever degree of coexistence there was between Israel and the inhabitants of the occupied territories. He went on to declare that

> blowing up houses and other sanctions are certainly part of that overall policy... and just as necessary for coexistence in the future.[60]

Legal justification for the policy of demolition has been sought by Israel in the continued applicability of the Palestine Mandate Emergency Regulations of 1945. Regulation 119 permits demolition of any house, some or all of whose occupants have been found by the local military commander

> to have contravened regulations or attempted to do so, or aided others, or have been party to the actions of others in contravention of the regulations.[61]

It is sometimes suggested that Israel is entitled, or even obliged, to keep in force these regulations (said to have been maintained by Jordan as part of its law) by virtue of Article 43 of the Hague Regulations which, as discussed above, requires the occupier to respect, 'unless absolutely prevented', the laws in force in the occupied territory. This uncharacteristic scrupulosity in adhering strictly to the letter of the Hague Regulations provokes two basic objections.

The first is that, in the words of the standard English treatise on international law,

> in the exceptional cases in which the law of the occupied State is such as to flout and shock elementary concepts of justice and the rule of law, the occupying State must be deemed entitled to disregard it.[62]

After the 1945 Emergency Regulations were promulgated in Palestine, they were greeted in the Jewish legal community with general denunciation. At a meeting in 1946 of the Jewish Lawyers' Association, a future Israeli Supreme Court justice stated:

> as lawyers, we are especially concerned because they violate the basic principles of law, justice, and jurisprudence... The defense regulations abolish the rights of the individual and grant unlimited power to the administration.[63]

Yaacov Shimshon Shapiro, later to be Minister of Justice in the Israeli government that established the military administration in

52

the occupied territories after the 1967 war, said of the Regulations at that meeting:

> The established order in Palestine since the defense [emergency] regulations is unparalleled in any civilized country. Even in Nazi Germany there were no such laws...
> It is our duty to tell the whole world that the defense regulations passed by the government in Palestine destroy the very foundations of justice in this land.[64]

The Lawyers' Association then adopted resolutions declaring in part that

> The powers granted the authorities under the emergency regulations deprive the Palestine citizen of the fundamental rights of man

and that

> These regulations undermine law and justice, and constitute a grave danger to the life and liberty of the individual, establishing a rule of violence without any judicial control.[65]

The opinions of these eminent Jewish lawyers before their principles were influenced by the exercise of power over Arabs may be taken as strong support for the view that the Emergency Regulations do flout and shock elementary concepts of justice and the rule of law. Consequently, even if they were in fact kept in force by Jordan before 1967, the Emergency Regulations may nevertheless be disregarded by Israel, and, indeed, must be disregarded if the humanitarian provisions of the law of belligerent occupation are to be respected. The situation then existing would be that described by Lauterpacht in which the occupier is, in terms of Article 43 of the Hague Regulations, 'absolutely prevented' from 'administering laws and principles the application of which within occupied territory [is] utterly opposed to modern conceptions of the rule of law'.[66]

There is a second and distinct, but equally fundamental, objection to Israel's case. For, clearly, an occupier possesses only those rights and duties conferred by international law.[67] The occupier's right to maintain existing laws in force derives from Article 43 of the Hague Regulations which in general remain fully effective insofar as they have not been superseded by the Fourth Geneva Convention.[68] Thus, to understand the present effect of the Hague Regulations it is necessary to read them together with the Convention and apply the two documents consistently. Since Article 33 of the Fourth Geneva Convention is absolute and admits of no exception or derogation, it would be incorrect to allow a derogation through an isolated reading of Article 43 of the Hague Regulations. Article 43 therefore cannot legitimately be interpreted as permitting what Article 33 of the Convention unequivocally and absolutely forbids.

The same reasoning applies when interpreting the various provisions of the Fourth Convention itself. As we have seen, while Article 33 absolutely forbids collective penalties and reprisals against protected persons and their property, Article 53 permits destruction of private property 'where such destruction is rendered absolutely necessary by military operations'. The I.C.R.C. Commentary indicates that Article 33's prohibition of reprisals, because it is absolute and mandatory, 'cannot be interpreted as containing tacit reservations with regard to military necessity'.[69] The same may be said of Article 33 in its entirety. Thus, Article 33's protections cannot be taken as limited by Article 53's exception for military necessity. On the contrary, that exception – in any case, to be construed narrowly on principle – must be read as limited by those protections. Consequently, destruction of private property for purposes of collective punishment or reprisals is not permitted by the Convention even in a case where 'military necessity' might be argued.

The question then comes down to whether demolition of houses in which many people live is under Article 33 a collective penalty or a reprisal or both. Defenders of the Israeli position generally deny that the Israeli authorities inflict collective penalties in any situation. Brigadier Ben-Eliezer, military governor of the West Bank, has acknowledged, however, that

> It's true that there have been cases where we've had no choice but to use collective measures.[70]

To exclude house demolitions from such 'collective measures' it would seem necessary to argue that the many innocent people affected by demolitions are undergoing not collective penalties but merely collective suffering which is an inevitable by-product of an individual penalty. This begs the question, however. For it is perfectly obvious that the operative element of any penalty is the suffering it inflicts. This fact reduces the counter-argument to a question of arid semantics which revolves around whether suffering knowingly and deliberately inflicted escapes being a

54

'penalty' merely because the actor chooses to claim it is aimed at someone else. Furthermore, there is in any event nothing at all inevitable about the suffering of the innocent in such a situation, since the Israeli authorities could follow the obligatory basic principle of Article 33 – that responsibility is individual and personal – and inflict only punishment that applies to the person found guilty of terrorism. Absent such selectivity, house demolitions can hardly avoid being classified as collective penalties.

In any case, it has never been demonstrated that blowing up an uncle's house punishes his nephew or that demolishing a landlord's building penalizes mainly – or even at all – the tenant suspect.

Objections like these provoke the suspicion that the deterrent effect of house demolitions – all along admitted by the Israeli authorities to be a major justification – is in fact the primary purpose of demolition. The situation then prevailing would be little distinguishable from that described by the I.C.R.C. Commentary where the occupier resorts to intimidatory measures 'to terrorise the population... to prevent hostile acts'.[71] Can there be any substantial doubt about that conclusion in view of Gen. Orly's statement that demolition is necessary for 'co-existence' between Israel and the Palestinians of the occupied teritories? Since the individual perpetrators of guerrilla acts are regularly sentenced to long prison terms, Gen. Orly could hardly have been advocating demolition to promote 'co-existence' with them. Therefore, 'co-existence' – which, one notes, was Gen. Orly's *sole* justification for demolitions – could be directed only towards other Palestinians who have not been charged or convicted for any crime. In these circumstances house demolitions would be prohibited by being 'measures of intimidation' under Article 33. On the basis of that illegality they could then in turn be classified also in some instances at least as reprisals: that is, acts contrary to law undertaken against innocent protected persons for the purpose of ensuring cessation of hostile acts committed not by those persons but by others who may be expected to be influenced by observing the suffering of the innocent.[72] As reprisals, demolitions would constitute a third illegality under Article 33.

If the Israeli high command believe, as maintained by Gen. Orly, that demolitions are 'necessary for co-existence in the future', there can be no doubt that the Israeli security forces,

55

given *carte blanche* by the Plan's security provisions, will feel free to continue that particular illegality after the establishment of autonomy. Another item is thereby added to the already long list of international legal violations that Article 11 of the Begin Plan would sanction.

5   *Interference with the work of international humanitarian organizations*

As noted above, Israel is forbidden by Article 47 of the Fourth Geneva Convention to deny protected persons the 'benefits' of the Convention. One of these benefits is the presence and activity of humanitarian organizations in occupied territory as provided for by Article 10, which reads:

> The provisions of the present Convention constitute no obstacle to the humanitarian activities which the International Committee of the Red Cross or any other impartial humanitarian organization may, subject to the consent of the Parties to the conflict concerned, undertake for the protection of civilian persons and for their relief.

The effects of this Article are manifold. It is, first, a sweeping affirmation that nothing in the Convention may be taken as implying an obstacle to humanitarian activities. Secondly, it recognizes the international legal position not only of the International Committee of the Red Cross but of 'any other impartial humanitarian organization', international or local. Furthermore, it indicates that the permitted humanitarian activities include not merely relief but also 'protection of civilian persons'.

The I.C.R.C. Commentary makes clear that such protection may relate to the whole fabric of the Convention's benefits and may take the form of 'representation, interventions, suggestions and *practical measures* affecting the protection accorded under the Convention'[73] [emphasis supplied]. Such protective activities 'may be of any kind and carried out in any manner, even indirect, compatible with the sovereignty and security of the State in question'.[74]

The Commentary refers to the consent provision of Article 10 in this way:

> A belligerent Power can obviously not be *obliged* to tolerate in

its territory activities of any kind by any foreign organization.[75] [emphasis supplied]

As an application of the general international legal principle of state sovereignty within state territory (i.e. territorial supremacy), this comment may be correct as regards those parts of the Convention relating solely to treatment of aliens within a state's own territory. Indeed, it is only as an application of that principle that it could be correct. The principle, however, clearly does not apply in occupied territory where 'the occupant in no wise acquires sovereignty over such territory through the mere fact of having occupied it'[76] but rather possesses merely 'a temporary right of administration'[77] subject in all respects to the requirements of international law. That being the case, the Commentary's observation cannot be assumed to reach the work of international humanitarian organizations in occupied territory.

The Commentary emphasizes that the organizations referred to in Article 10 must be impartial. It points out that impartiality does not mean mathematical equality and may consist in the organization's being willing to offer its services to all the belligerent parties.[78] Article 10 should not be construed to require impartiality between violators of the Convention and their victims considered as suffering human beings, for such impartiality between legality and illegality would significantly vitiate the Convention's protective force.

Having recognized the role of humanitarian organizations, the Convention goes on in Article 30 to provide for the access of protected persons to them. Those persons

> shall have every facility for making application to... any organization that might assist them.[79]

The Article confers on the organizations an important right of their own:

> These several organizations shall be granted all facilities for that purpose, within the bounds set by military or security considerations.

The Commentary points out that protected persons must be 'furnished with the support they require to obtain their rights; they would otherwise be helpless from a legal point of view in relation to the Power in whose hands they are'.[80] It emphasizes further how important it is that a protected person should be able to rely on the 'moral support' of interested organizations and not merely the 'goodwill' of the occupying power.[81] Consequently, facilitating and promoting – not merely permitting – the work of such organizations is incumbent upon the occupying power.[82] The right of organizations to receive such facilities is limited only by the occupier's military and security – but not his political – considerations.

These general observations are appropriate background for evaluating the campaign in 1979 by Israeli military and civilian officials against a number of American humanitarian organizations operating in the occupied territories.[83] Interference in their work hindered some of these organizations in carrying on various community development programmes, notably on the West Bank,[84] but, significantly, the public campaign opened with an attack on the legal aid work of the American Friends Service Committee (A.F.S.C.).

The privately-funded A.F.S.C., in addition to operating a social service programme in Israel, has for several years run 'a modest legal aid center in East Jerusalem' which provided 'defense lawyers on request for Arabs accused of security offenses' and latterly helped 'Arabs fight civil actions against Israeli land expropriation and requisition orders'.[85] At the hearing in November 1978 on the *Beit El* settlement case referred to above, the Israeli State Attorney remarked to the judges of the High Court of Justice that, when 'confronted with a rash of appeals like this, one gets the feeling there is some guiding hand, and a political interest in embarrassing the Israeli government'[86] in the post-Camp David negotiations about which the Israeli government felt considerable political sensitivity. This was considered an allusion to the A.F.S.C.[87] and an attempt to prejudice the Court against the landowners' case. Some months later, after several newspaper and broadcast 'exposés' of the A.F.S.C. and the other American organizations, a 'well-placed source in the military government' gave it out that the A.F.S.C. had provided legal aid in at least one 'purely political' case and was consequently being advised to 'steer clear of political activities' in the occupied territories.[88] On July 4, 1979, the *Jerusalem Post* reported that the Israeli Social Affairs Ministry had asked the A.F.S.C. to 'stop giving legal advice' to Arabs on the West Bank because of 'serious breaches' by the organization of its agreement to perform humanitarian activities. On the following day, however, the *Jerusalem Post* quoted the Minister of Social Affairs as declaring:

> We do not oppose the extension of legal aid to those in need of it... so long as the legal aid is not abused for political purposes.

The A.F.S.C. was reported to have retained a lawyer to clarify its status.[89]

This incident is a significant revelation of the attitude of the Israeli authorities towards the rights possessed by Palestinians under the Fourth Geneva Convention.

In the Beit El case, Israeli civilian settlement was opposed by the Palestinian plaintiffs as contrary *inter alia* to the prohibition of population transfer contained in Article 49 of the Convention. The plaintiff landowners had a clear interest in enforcing that provision, since its violation through establishment of a civilian settlement on land seized from them affected their rights directly. As the I.C.R.C. Commentary notes, the relevant provision of Article 49 gives protected persons a 'valuable safeguard' against worsening of their economic situation and endangering of their separate existence as a race.[90] The right not to have such civilian transfers onto their land was thus secured directly to the plaintiffs by Article 49.

Indeed, as the Commentary indicates in connection with the non-derogation of rights provisions in the Convention's Articles 7 and 8, 'the whole system of rules under the Convention'[91] confers rights directly on protected persons. The Commentary goes on to declare that 'to assert that a person has a right is to say that he possesses ways and means of having that right respected'.[92] The ways and means provided to protect rights under the Convention are, firstly, that the protected person on his own may 'employ any procedure available, however rudimentary, to demand respect for the Convention's terms'.[93] Secondly, the protected person may benefit from the presence and activity of humanitarian organizations under Article 10 and exercise his right, under Article 30, to apply 'to any organization that might assist' him. Such an organization may respond under Article 10 by undertaking, in the Commentary's words, 'practical measures affecting the protection accorded under the Convention',[94] including assisting the protected person acting in accordance with Article 8 to employ available procedures – judicial and other – to demand respect for the rights conferred by the Convention. Precisely because the Fourth Geneva Convention is, in its entirety, a charter for human rights and humanitarian duties,[95] assistance to vindicate any of those rights through the ways and means authorized by the Convention necessarily responds to the Convention's humanitarian imperatives.

The conclusion then must be that the Palestinian landowners in the Beit El case had a right to bring suit in the High Court to stop civilian settlement and to seek assistance in that litigation – and outside it – from any interested humanitarian organization. Such an organization in turn had a right to give this assistance and to demand from the Israeli authorities that they should facilitate and promote its work. Such assistance within the scope of the Convention could not legitimately be subject to objections arising out of Israeli political – as distinct from military or security – considerations.

In the case of A.F.S.C., it is clear from examination of the State Attorney's remarks to the Court in the Beit El case and of the later accusations of A.F.S.C. 'political' activities that Israeli interference was not founded on justifications acceptable under the Convention. Indeed, insofar as the Israeli authorities fail to positively facilitate and promote legal aid seeking vindication of Convention rights, Israel is in violation of the Convention.

It is equally clear that in autonomy under the Plan, when Israel could claim to have been granted broader 'security' powers than she now possesses under international law, the question of how and with whose aid Palestinians in the occupied territories would be able to maintain their legal rights would be all the more pressing. Previous Israeli interference with humanitarian legal aid work may be taken as a reliable indication of the direction matters would move once the Israeli version of autonomy were instituted.

But if the Plan would perpetuate human rights violations on the level of individuals, it would also promote large-scale violations through the transformation in Palestinian society and economy being wrought by Israeli settlement in preparation for annexation of the occupied territories. These central faults, and their far-reaching implications, are considered next.

1 Cf. ENCYCLOPEDIA BRITANNICA (1973 ed.) article on 'Police'.
2 VON GLAHN, THE OCCUPATION OF ENEMY TERRITORY 43 (1957).
3 Begin Plan, Article 10.
4 GERSON, ISRAEL, THE WEST BANK AND INTERNATIONAL LAW 7.
5 *Id.*, referring to Article 47 of the Fourth Geneva Convention.
6 Gen. Ass. Res. 2200, 21 U.N. G.A.O.R., Supp. 16 (U.N. Doc. A/6316) pp.52–58.
7 GREIG, INTERNATIONAL LAW 812 (2nd ed.).
8 Text in COUNCIL OF EUROPE, COLLECTED TEXTS 1–19 (9th ed., 1974).
9 European Convention on Human Rights, Article 19.
10 The facts recited here are taken from the Affidavit in the Beit El Case on behalf of the Minister of Defence by Major-General Avraham Orly, at that time co-ordinator in the Ministry of Defence for operations in the occupied territories. This Affidavit will hereinafter be referred to as the 'Government Affidavit' and will be quoted in an unofficial English translation from the Hebrew. The Beit El Case was docketed in the High Court of Justice as No. 606/78.
11 Dunbar, 'Military Necessity in War Crimes Trials', quoted in X WHITEMAN, DIGEST OF INTERNATIONAL LAW 308.
12 Downey, 'The Law of War and Military Necessity', 47 A.J.I.L. 251, 254, quoted in X WHITEMAN, DIGEST OF INTERNATIONAL LAW 305.
13 O'Brien, 'Legitimate Military Necessity in Nuclear War', 11 YEARBOOK OF WORLD POLITY 35, 67, quoted in X WHITEMAN, DIGEST OF INTERNATIONAL LAW 316–317.
14 C. FENWICK, INTERNATIONAL LAW 655 (4th ed., 1965).
15 Hague Regulations, Article 22.
16 II LAUTERPACHT-OPPENHEIM, INTERNATIONAL LAW 233 (7th ed.).
17 *Id.*, at 233, note 2.
18 O'Brien, note 13 *supra*, quoted at X Whiteman 316.

19 Cf. Hague Regulations, Article 42: territory is considered occupied 'when it is placed under the authority of the hostile army'.

20 III BRITISH MANUAL OF MILITARY LAW: THE LAW OF WAR ON LAND 142 (1958 ed.). Cf. UNITED STATES DEPARTMENT OF THE ARMY FIELD MANUAL FM 27-10 THE LAW OF LAND WARFARE 139 (1956).

21 N.Y. Times, June 14, 1979, p. A3, cols. 1–6.

22 N.Y. Times, May 9, 1979, p. A11, col. 1.

23 I.C.R.C. COMMENTARY 337.

24 *Id.*, at 207.

25 Jerusalem Post Int'l Ed., Oct. 7–13, 1979, p.14.

26 *Id.*

27 *Id.*

28 *See* Lesch, 'Israeli Deportations of Palestinians from the West Bank and the Gaza Strip, 1967–1978', JOURNAL OF PALESTINE STUDIES, No.30, winter 1979, at 101–112 *and* No.31, spring 1979, at 81–112.

29 *See*, I.C.R.C. COMMENTARY 279, particularly note 3.

30 *See*, N.Y. Times, May 1, 1979, p. A3, cols. 1–3.

31 Quoted in Washington Post News Service Report by T.R. Reid and Edward Cody *reprinted* in the Jerusalem Post, Feb. 8, 1979, p.1.

32 *Id.*

33 I.C.R.C. COMMENTARY 204.

34 Cf. N.Y. Times, May 1, 1979, p. A3, cols. 1–3; *and* Cody and Reid report cited in note 31, *supra*.

35 Eur. Court H.R., Series A, Judgment of January 18, 1978 Paragraph 159.

36 *See*, for example, Jerusalem Post editorial, May 8, 1979; Anthony Lewis in N.Y. Times, June 4, 1979; MIDDLE EAST INTERNATIONAL 25 May, 1979; Washington Post, June 1, 1979; U.S. NEWS AND WORLD REPORT, Aug. 6, 1979.

37 William Claiborne reporting in the Washington Post, June 1, 1979.

38 I.C.R.C. COMMENTARY 213.

39 N.Y. Times, Oct. 16, 1979, p. A5, cols. 1–6.

40 Jerusalem Post, Feb. 5, 1979, p.8.

41 *See*, Boston Globe, July 8, 1979, p.19.

42 *Id.*
43 *Id.*
44 *Id.*
45 Jer. Post Int'l Ed., Aug. 12–18, 1979, p.9.
46 *Id.*
47 *Id.*
48 I.C.R.C. COMMENTARY 225.
49 *Id.*, at 225–226.
50 *Id.*, at 227–228
51 TEVETH, THE CURSED BLESSING 243.
52 *Id.*, at 244.
53 *Id.*, at 352.
54 *Id.*, at 326.
55 *Id.*, at 313.
56 *Id.*, at 244.
57 *Id.*, at 300.
58 Jerusalem Post, Jan. 31, 1979, p.3.
59 Jerusalem Post, Feb. 6, 1979, p.10.
60 *Id.*
61 TEVETH, op. cit., at 243.
62 II LAUTERPACHT-OPPENHEIM 446.
63 Quoted in JIRYIS, THE ARABS IN ISRAEL 11 (1976 ed.).
64 *Id.*, at 12.
65 *Id.*, at 13.
66 II LAUTERPACHT-OPPENHEIM 447.
67 Cf. II LAUTERPACHT-OPPENHEIM 434.
68 Cf. II LAUTERPACHT-OPPENHEIM 451–452.
69 I.C.R.C. COMMENTARY 228.
70 Jer. Post Int'l Ed., Oct. 7–13, 1979, p.14.
71 I.C.R.C. COMMENTARY 226.
72 Cf. I.C.R.C. COMMENTARY 227–228. On reprisals in general *see* II LAUTERPACHT-OPPENHEIM 561–565. On the progressive development of the law on this point by the Fourth Geneva Convention, *see* II LAUTERPACHT-OPPENHEIM 443–444.
73 I.C.R.C. COMMENTARY 97.
74 *Id.*, at 98.
75 *Id.*
76 II LAUTERPACHT-OPPENHEIM 433.
77 *Id.*, at 436.

78 I.C.R.C. COMMENTARY 97.
79 Fourth Geneva Convention, Article 30.
80 I.C.R.C. COMMENTARY 214.
81 *Id.*, at 215.
82 *Id.*, at 218.
83 *See*, THE ECONOMIST, June 9, 1979, p.77; Boston Globe, July 5, 1979.
84 Boston Globe, July 5, 1979.
85 *Id.*
86 Jerusalem Post, Nov. 24, 1978, p.2.
87 N.Y. Times, July 5, 1979, p. A5, col.1.
88 Jerusalem Post, June 12, 1979.
89 N.Y. Times, July 5, 1979, p. A5, col.1.
90 I.C.R.C. COMMENTARY 283.
91 *Id.*, at 78.
92 *Id.*
93 *Id.*, at 79.
94 *Id.*, at 97.
95 *See* PICTET, HUMANITARIAN LAW AND THE PROTECTION OF WAR VICTIMS 17.

4 Israel's Territorial Supremacy under the Plan: Legitimation of Settlement and Annexation

An Israeli Cabinet minister observed several years ago that the 'struggle over settlement is an organic part of the struggle over the peace borders',[1] by which he may be understood to have meant that the existence of settlements in the occupied territories is intended to determine how large a slice of those areas Israel will be able to incorporate behind its expanded 'peace borders'. The political link between settlement and annexation could hardly have been made clearer, but it remained for the Israeli autonomy Plan to attempt elaboration of a legal mechanism whereby that link and its consequences could claim legitimation.

As will be seen, the Israeli argument for the legality of its settlements is largely based on the denial of any other party's sovereign rights over the occupied territories. In its case for annexation, Israel then takes the next logical step and asserts its own rights of sovereignty there. In providing explicitly for both settlement and annexation, the Israeli autonomy scheme thus raises the fundamental issue: what right, if any, under international law would entitle Israel to claim respect for, and to effectuate, her views on sovereignty? Israel's legal position will be seen to rest almost entirely on her use of force to seize those territories in 1967 and maintain her control of them since then. The international law governing the use of force, and the implications of that law for attempts in the Plan and elsewhere to legitimate the consequences of Israel's use of force, must therefore be examined in some detail.

This chapter considers each of these areas of legal concern and the significance for the peace process of the interrelated illegalities involved.

A SETTLEMENTS

Article 20 of the Begin Plan provided that 'residents' of Israel would be entitled to acquire land and settle in occupied territories and also that Arab residents of those territories, provided they became Israeli citizens under Article 14 of the Begin Plan, would be entitled to acquire land and settle in Israel.

Article 20 clearly does not place the residents of Israel and the Arab residents of the occupied territories on a level of equality and it does not deal with the question of settlement on a basis of reciprocity. The category of persons who may settle in the territories is very broad (including anyone the government of Israel may choose to regard as a 'resident', as, for example, new Jewish immigrants from the Soviet Union[2]). In contrast, the category of Arabs who may own land and settle in Israel is drawn not from the Palestinian diaspora but, under Article 14, only from that presumptively limited group of territories' residents who wish to declare allegiance to Israel. Thus, although Israeli residents would enjoy in the occupied territories unrestricted rights such as are usually reserved only for nationals of a country within its own borders, the opportunity for Palestinian settlement within Israel would not in any way lessen Israel's authority or jurisdiction within its territory. There can be no doubt which party is placed at an advantage by Article 20.

But larger questions than that of inequality are also raised by Article 20. They relate to the legality of the settlements themselves.

1 Illegality of Settlements Absent the Plan

Two opposing views on the legality of Israeli settlements in the areas occupied in 1967 have been put forward. Both views have been well canvassed elsewhere and need not be repeated in detail. Brief examination of them is necessary here, however, to place Article 20 in perspective.

The view which holds such settlements to be illegal is based on application of the Hague Regulations of 1907 and the Fourth Geneva Convention of 1949.

United States Ambassador Charles Yost in 1969 put before the Security Council the general objection to Israeli occupation policy in these words:

> Among the provisions of international law which bind Israel, as they would bind any occupier, are the provisions that...an occupier may not confiscate or destroy private property...the occupier must maintain the occupied area as intact and unaltered as possible, without interfering with the customary life of the area...[3]

This statement of the American view was reaffirmed by President Carter in the Camp David package of documents,[4] and the State Department Legal Adviser has set out the American argument for this position. It is based primarily on Articles 42 to 56 of the Hague Regulations and Article 49 of the Fourth Geneva Convention.[5] Regarding the limits imposed by the Hague Regulations, the Legal Adviser concluded that Israeli settlements in occupied territory

> do not appear to be consistent with these limits...in that they do not seem to be intended to be of limited duration or established to provide orderly government of the territories and, though some may serve incidental security purposes, they do not appear to be required to meet military needs during the occupation.[6]

As to the separate and distinct argument based on the prohibition contained in Article 49 of the Fourth Geneva Convention, the Legal Adviser found that Article applicable to any transfer by the occupant of parts of its own civilian population into the occupied territories 'whatever the objective and whether involuntary or voluntary'.[7]

This presentation of the general legal case against settlements cannot be taken as exhaustively comprehensive. It neglects, for example, the particular, but not unique, violations of international law that laid the basis for Mevo Horon settlement in the Latrun area. There, following wholesale Israeli expulsion of the indigenous Arab inhabitants, the Arab villages of Yalu, Imwas, and Beit Nuba were totally obliterated by the occupying Israeli forces after the cessation of fighting in 1967. Mevo Horon was subsequently established in the area so cleared.[8]

Nevertheless, the Legal Adviser's statement outlined the basic condemnation of Israel's settlement policy and practice, and it is in the light of that condemnation that Israel has had to enunciate its justifications.

Israel's defence of settlements

Israel has adopted two basic defences of its settlement policy.

The first claims that settlement is legal because justified by security considerations in Israel's case. The implications and weaknesses of the security argument have been discussed in Chapter 3 above.

The second line of defence attempts to avoid the difficulties encountered over the first by denying the obligatory applicability of the laws of belligerent occupation and arguing for the *sui generis* nature of Israel's position, particularly on the West Bank.[9] This so-called 'missing reversioner'[10] argument, which is the basic premise of the Israeli case, and the conclusion drawn from it were stated in 1971 by the then Israeli Attorney General Meir Shamgar in these words:

> The whole idea of the restriction of military government powers is based on the assumption that there had been a sovereign who was ousted and that he had been a legitimate sovereign...
>
> Israel never recognized the rights of Egypt and Jordan to the territory occupied by them till 1967...
>
> ...in the interpretation most favorable to the Kingdom of Jordan her legal standing in the West Bank was at most that of a belligerent occupant following an unlawful invasion [and not that of the legitimate sovereign]...
>
> The same conclusion would apply to the Gaza Strip which was regarded by the U.A.R. government as territory under military occupation, and that Government never even raised the claim that it had any legal rights to the territory.
>
> The territorial position is thus *sui generis*...[11]

The implications of a *sui generis* territorial position for the question of annexation are considered in section C, below, when examining Israel's 'defensive conquest-better title' claim. This section will look at the argument's relevance to the applicability of the law of belligerent occupation.

It has been recognized that the Fourth Geneva Convention was to a considerable extent declaratory of customary international law's supplementary development of the Hague Regulations in the interest of individuals.[12] Shamgar is therefore incorrect when he implies that the law of belligerent occupation aims solely to protect the interests of an 'ousted sovereign'. Article 4 of the Convention makes clear that that document's protection runs to persons, whose rights exist independently of the actions or positions of States (Articles 7 and 11) and whose rights cannot be limited or renounced even by agreement of the protected persons themselves (Article 8). In explicating Article 8, which indicates that protected persons have '*rights* secured *to them*' by the Convention (emphasis supplied), the I.C.R.C. Fourth Convention Commentary notes that the promulgation of the Convention was, with one exception, 'the first time that a set of international regulations has been devoted not to state interests, but solely to the protection of the individual'.[13] The United Nations Security Council, in paragraph 2 of its Resolution 237 of June 14, 1967,[14] specifically recognized the humanitarian character of the Fourth Convention and recommended scrupulous respect of its principles by all governments involved in the 1967 war. Furthermore, the Resolution's preamble may be understood to imply that the Convention's provisions protect 'essential and inalienable human rights',[15] that is, rights of an indelible character which arise from fundamental international law.[16] In this spirit, the I.C.R.C. Commentary interprets Article 8 of the convention as entitling protected persons 'to claim the protection of the Convention, not as a favour, but as a right'.[17] The protections afforded by the Convention (including those of Article 49) clearly do not depend on the existence of an ousted legitimate sovereign.

Sovereignty over Gaza and the West Bank

But, even were the existence of an ousted sovereign necessary for the application of the laws of belligerent occupation, what is the basis for the implicit Israeli assumption that that sovereign must be Jordan, or Egypt, so that, failing Jordanian or Egyptian legitimacy, there is no other sovereign? Although the rationale for this assumption is not stated, one may reasonably suppose that it is grounded in an unwillingness to accept the obvious alternative, i.e., Palestinian sovereignty. That alternative's legal viability has been examined by two scholars who, starting from opposite premises, reach the same conclusion. The process of their reasoning deserves consideration.

Henry Cattan, noting that Article 22 of the League of Nations Covenant accepted that '[c]ertain communities formerly belonging to the Turkish Empire have reached a stage of development where their existence as independent nations can be provisionally recognized',[18] finds that the Palestinian 'A' Mandate given to the United Kingdom by the League in 1922 violated this, and other, provisions of Article 22. The Mandate was thus, in effect, *'ultra vires'* or 'unconstitutional', since even a 'legislative' act of the League of Nations Council could not override the constitutive law of the League itself.[19] The Mandate violated the Covenant in that it did not promote the interests of the indigenous inhabitants of Palestine (the overwhelming majority of whom were Arabs) but established, contrary to the wishes of the inhabitants, a Mandatory government whose purpose was to impose on Palestine the concept of the Jewish National Home rather than to set up an administration giving temporary advice and assistance to the inhabitants in preparation for that independence envisaged by Article 22.[20] That Article 22 'recognized' the existence of the relevant communities, including Palestine, as independent nations had the effect that

> Palestine had become a separate and independent political entity...and was now possessed of its own statehood and sovereignty, [although] its people were prevented from the exercise of effective sovereignty.[21]

Sovereignty would thus have remained in the community over whom the Mandate was exercized and could not have vested in the Mandatory Power nor in the League of Nations itself. What the League did not possess it could not have passed on to its successor organization, the United Nations. Consequently, in Cattan's view, the attempt by the United Nations in the General Assembly's Partition Resolution of 1947 effectively to divide sovereignty over Palestine was invalid and void since

> Neither individually, nor collectively, could the members of the UN alienate, reduce, or impair the sovereignty of the people of Palestine, or dispose of their territory, or destroy by partition the territorial integrity of their country.[22]

70

Since belligerent occupation also does not produce a transfer of sovereignty,[23] Cattan concludes that the Palestinians' 'sovereignty survives despite the situation created by force in Palestine'.[24]

In an interesting examination of the nature of Israel's occupation in the West Bank,[25] Dr. Allan Gerson, in contrast to Cattan, predicates his analysis on the assumption that the Mandate over Palestine was legal.[26] However, that legality existed by virtue of, and was circumscribed by, the League of Nations' concept that each mandate territory was under tutelage, or in trust, to the Mandatory for the benefit of the inhabitants of the territory. Thus a Mandate conferred no title or sovereignty on the Mandatory but left sovereignty 'retained by the beneficiary people...in a state of suspension'.[27] The Palestine Mandate, although granting in Gerson's words, 'special rights...to a people constituting a minority of only 12 per cent of the entire population',[28] did not give that people exclusive rights which it could claim even in the face of the Palestinians' refusal to become a minority in their own country.[29] This limitation on the rights of the Jewish people arose, Gerson suggests, from the sequence of events preceding the granting of the Mandate by the League Council. He argues that, after the Zionist Executive accepted the Churchill White Paper's statement that 'development of the Jewish National Home' did not mean 'the imposition of a Jewish nationality upon the inhabitants of Palestine as a whole',[30] this White Paper interpretation of the meaning of the Balfour Declaration became the understanding of the Mandate's effect which the League Council must be taken to have considered applicable when it approved the terms of the Mandate.[31] Consequently, for full sovereignty over all of Palestine to have vested in the Jewish people, all the inhabitants of Palestine would presumably have had to accept 'Jewish nationality' (whatever that might have meant). Failing such acceptance, full sovereignty could not have vested in the Jewish people. Since, however, the Mandate created, in Gerson's view, such Jewish interests in Palestine that sovereignty could also not have vested entirely in the Arab majority, sovereignty 'both from a pragmatic and a legal viewpoint'[32] became divisible. Hence, '[p]artition... was... the only legal alternative in which the rights of the parties to the Mandate could be reconciled'.[33] Gerson then seems to suggest that the unique legitimacy of partition obviated the problem of illegality in the Partition Resolution of 1947 which became merely a statement of the existing legal situation and did not unlawfully create new legal obligations or abolish existing rights.[34] The Resolution, in allotting sovereignty partly to the Jews and partly to the Palestinians, was only implementing a pre-existing legal solution produced by the logic of events. As the embodiment of that uniquely valid solution, the Resolution was binding upon the parties.[35] 'Consequently', says Gerson, 'sovereignty in the West Bank vested in the Palestinian Arabs in 1947'.[36]

After examining events in the following twenty years, Dr Gerson concludes that, even though, as claimed by Israel, Jordan may not have been the legitimate sovereign of the West Bank before 1967, Israel derived from that fact no proper claim of sovereignty. The West Bank neither was *res nullius* (i.e., 'an asset susceptible of acquisition but presently under the ownership or sovereignty of no legal person'[37]) nor was subject to any legitimate latent right of sovereignty of Israel's.[38] Hence, the Palestinian inhabitants of the West Bank retain in a state of suspension the legitimate sovereignty over their area.[39] This conclusion presumably also applies at least to Gaza, which was within the area allotted to the Palestinians under the Partition Resolution.

Thus, whether one denies or accepts the legality of the Palestine Mandate (and hence indirectly the legitimacy of Israel's statehood), one arrives at the same conclusion with regard to sovereignty over the areas of Palestine currently occupied by Israel. Such sovereignty remains with the Palestinians, and consequently Israeli claims based on a hypothetical failure of Arab sovereignty are invalid.

Cattan and Gerson would differ, however, over the legal consequences of this conclusion. For Cattan, Palestinian sovereignty in abeyance leaves Israel in the position of a belligerent occupant and therefore fully bound by the relevant international law to make no changes of any sort in the *status quo ante* 1967.[40] Dr Gerson, on the other hand, appears to believe that, although the Palestinians possess sovereignty over the territories, they have never effectuated their sovereign power so as to establish governmental structures and laws which Israel must maintain in existence pending Palestinian exercise of sovereignty at the termination of the occupation.[41] Therefore, in Gerson's view, Israel 'would not be barred from implementing any changes in the existing laws or institutions *provided such amendments were in the best interests of the inhabitants*[42] (emphasis supplied). Yet, even by this analysis, Israel would be barred from introducing in her own interest changes that had the effect of infringing Palestinian legal rights, since it is clear *ex hypothesi* that loss or infringement of rights cannot be in the inhabitants' best interests. Furthermore, experience and commonsense support the observation of the I.C.R.C. Commentary that '[w]hen a State offers persons in its hands the choice of another status, such a step is usually dictated by its own interest'.[43] Such considerations motivated the absolute non-renunciation of rights provision in the Fourth Geneva Convention[44] and they militate against any reading of international law that would permit Israel to disregard or avoid the substantive restrictions imposed on her by the law of belligerent occupation.

The conclusion must be that, even if the existence of a legitimate sovereign were necessary to invoke the Geneva Convention, such a sovereign is present in the Palestinian people so that the Convention is fully applicable to the Israeli occupation. Israel is therefore obliged to cause no infringement of protected Palestinian social, economic, human, and political rights.

The adverse impact of settlements

It is sometimes suggested that Israeli settlements, with their relatively small populations, do not produce such political or other changes in the character of the occupied territories as the Fourth Convention's Article 49 is said to be intended to prevent.[45] Aside from arguments based on Article 49's absolute and unrestricted character, it may be objected also that this defence is essentially a temporary one whose factual basis is being steadily eroded as new settlements are established. An investigative commission appointed by the United Nations found that there were, as of mid-1979, 17 settlements in and around Jerusalem and 62 in other parts of the West Bank, with a total population of approximately 90,000 settlers.[46] In September 1979, it was reported that Matityahu Drobles, head of the Jewish Agency's land settlement department, had recommended in 1978 the establishment of an additional 46 settlements in the West Bank to accommodate 16,000 Israeli families by late 1983.[47] Drobles later proposed a further six settlements to ring the West Bank's largest Arab city, Nablus,[48] bringing the number of new colonies to 52 – nearly doubling the existing total on the West Bank. On November 11, 1979, the Israeli Cabinet approved further settlements in principle, with a special ministerial committee to consider, *inter alia*, a proposal by the Minister of Agriculture to create 16 new settlements in the 1979-1980 Hebrew calendar year.[49] Shortly thereafter, plans were announced to triple the Jewish population of the West Bank by the end of 1981 through a $100,000,000 settlement expansion programme.[50] Clearly the pace of these activities is such that an argument based on minimizing the significance of the extent of settlements is fast losing any relation with reality.

But even conceptually the argument's basic assumption – that settlements per se do not change the character of the occupied territories – seems itself ill-founded. Particularly in the political sphere the claim appears untenable in view of official Israeli pronouncements on the matter. Former Foreign Minister Allon when in office said, for example:

> ...settlements are placed in strategically important areas along existing borderlines or in the vicinity of areas likely to become borderlines in the future...
> ...I'm striving for a solution that would give us a complete country strategically and a complete country from a Jewish national standpoint...[51]

A head of the World Zionist Organization's Settlement Department declared: 'Our settlements have always established the facts of the map of Israel',[52] and the chairman of the previous government's ministerial committee for settlement affairs was even more precise:

> ...what we have accomplished from the six day war until now [June 1977] constitutes an extremely significant reality from a political, security and national point of view...
> ...The struggle over settlement is an organic part of the struggle over the peace borders...[53]

Thus, even under the Labour government, security concerns were already intertwined with motives of Jewish nationalism to encourage settlement that would promote Israeli territorial expansion.

During the period of the Begin administration a similar

74

combination of motives existed, as is evident in this extract from the Drobles Plan:

> 1 Settlement throughout the entire Land of Israel is for security and by right. A strip of settlements at strategic sites enhances both internal and external security alike, as well as making concrete and realizing [i.e., 'actualizing'] our right to Eretz-Israel.[54]

However, growing concern over the possibility of Palestinian autonomy in the wake of the Egyptian-Israeli negotiations following the Camp David agreements prompted Israeli officials to enunciate publicly a third specific purpose of settlement in addition to security and national territorial ambitions. Eliahu Ben-Elissar, director general of the Prime Minister's office indicated in July 1979 that the object of the Israeli settlement drive was to enlarge the West Bank's Jewish population to prevent 'Palestinian autonomy from ever developing into an independent Palestinian state'.[55] In effect, the purpose of settlements was to foreclose the central political option for the occupied territories.

Against this background of increasingly clear political motivation, the Israeli High Court of Justice in the autumn of 1979 ruled upon the legality of the Gush Emunim colony of Elon Moreh near Nablus.[56] The legal basis of the Court's judgement that establishment of the settlement contravened international law may conveniently be discussed below. The Court's findings of fact are significant in the present context, however.

The Court found on the basis of the evidence presented that the 'dominant' motivation in the creation of Elon Moreh was political and not military[57] and it accepted that the intention of the Gush Emunim settlers and of the Begin government was to create 'the Elon Moreh settlement as a permanent Jewish settlement, no less than Deganya or Netanya'.[58] The separate concurring opinion of Justice Bakhor went further to touch the status of settlements in general. He noted that historically in Israel the basis of colonization 'was always that the civilian settlements are permanent' and that 'the intent was to establish permanent settlements'.[59] He saw a 'contradiction' between seizure of land under temporary military occupation and the 'creation of permanent settlements'.[60]

In the aftermath of the High Court's decision, Gush Emunim leaders, apparently employing confrontation tactics,[61] announced that all their settlements had been politically motivated.[62]

Although the High Court may have been mainly concerned with settlement decisions reached under political pressure while the Gush Emunim leaders probably referred to settlement motivated by political goals, these aspects are clearly two sides of the same coin. The ultimately political repercussions in the occupied territories are implicit in both instances.

Some of those repercussions on the legal, demographic, social and economic character of the territories are spelled out in the Drobles Plan referred to above. After declaring that settlements are important for 'making concrete and realizing our right to Eretz-Israel', Drobles enunciated

> a settlement policy of blocs in homogeneous settlement areas which are mutually interrelated, this enabling, in time, the development of common services and means of production. Moreover, in the wake of the expansion and development of the community settlements, some of them may even combine, in the course of time, into an urban settlement.[63]

In effect, as settlements serve to entrench *de facto* Israeli territorial supremacy, they will also provide the cores of exclusive ('homogeneous') and ever-expanding Jewish enclaves which will develop a dynamic Jewish economy independent of the existing Arab economic structures and, inevitably, in competition with them for economic superiority. Urbanization will in time destroy the present generally rural character of the occupied territories, and, very likely, the indigenous Arab population will become an urban proletariat, as discussed in Chapter 2 above.

Indeed, the subordinate minority role envisaged by the Drobles Plan for the present Arab majority in the West Bank is plainly stated, as is the importance of siting settlements so as to atomize the Palestinian community and, implicitly, to undermine its solidarity:

> The disposition of the settlements must be carried out not only around the settlements of the minorities [e.g., the indigenous Palestinian majority], but also in between them, this in accordance with the settlement policy adopted in Galilee and in other parts of the country. Over the course of time, with or without peace, we will have to learn to live with the minorities and among them... Therefore the proposed settlement blocs are situated as a strip surrounding the (Judea and Samaria) ridge – starting from its western slopes from north to south,

and along its eastern slopes from south to north: both between the minorities population and around it.[64]

The indicated analogy between the Drobles proposals and settlement policy in Galilee is illuminating and disturbing. According to the *Jerusalem Post*,[65] settlement activity in Galilee over a period of several years has been 'spurred by the perception at the highest levels of government of the threat of an Arab-dominated Central Galilee'.[66] In addition to agricultural and industrial settlements inserted between existing Palestinian villages, Israeli policy in Galilee provides for *mitzpim* ('observation outposts') which

> are intended to be the nuclei of future settlements and are sited in quasi-military fashion in the mountains above the largest Arab villages...[67]

The new Jewish settlements were said by the *Post* to be less important as a means of changing the demographic balance in Galilee than for establishing a Jewish presence in the Arab areas. Nevertheless, the need for the *mitzpim* was said to be that overcrowded Arab villages had to be constantly under Jewish observation to prevent expansion of Arab building to accommodate the increasing Arab population. Clearly, if the *mitzpim* succeed in this purpose, the result will be that Arabs who do not wish to remain in inadequate village accommodations will have to leave the area altogether, joining in all probability the uprooted Arab proletariat in the larger towns. The *mitzpim* would thus have a direct effect on the local demographic balance as well as the social fabric of the Arab communities. When the Drobles Plan for the West Bank invokes settlement practices in Galilee, it thus calls up a precedent aimed quite deliberately at altering the character of the affected area.

Furthermore, the Drobles Plan notes that its implementation will allow dispersion of Israel's Jewish population 'from the densely populated urban strip of the coastal plain eastward to the presently empty areas of Judea and Samaria'.[68] Since the Drobles Plan is to be put into effect 'with or without peace', the proposed dispersion of the Jewish population might take place while the West Bank would be still under the protection of the Fourth Geneva Convention's Article 49 prohibition of population transfers into the occupied territories. In any event, this passage in the Drobles Plan may be taken to suggest that settlements are necessary better to accommodate the existing Jewish population, that in effect the existing population problem is the *raison d'être* of settlement. And yet Israel pursues a vigorous policy of promoting Jewish immigration, most notably that of the large Jewish community in the Soviet Union. Indeed, Zionist ideologues may be as deeply disturbed by the movement of existing Soviet Jews to the United States as they are by the inability of many other Soviet Jews to leave the U.S.S.R. at all, since great pressure is applied by Israel on all concerned in the emigration of Soviet Jews in order to see that those Jews be obliged to go to Israel rather than any other place they may instead prefer.[69] A possible explanation of this seeming paradox appeared in a debate of the Israeli Knesset in January 1979. The *Jerusalem Post* reported[70] on the debate in part as follows:

> Prof. Arens, chairman of the all-important Foreign Affairs and Defence Committee of the Knesset, said that a major settlement drive should be expedited, on the basis of land expropriations and the channelling of large numbers of immigrants.

Evidently, if large numbers of immigrants are unavailable, a major settlement drive (such as that envisaged in the Drobles Plan?) might prove very difficult or even impossible. Could it be, as Prof. Arens' proposal would suggest, that a current motive of large-scale immigration is to provide the necessary manpower for territorial expansion through settlements? It may well be the case that Israel absorbs immigrants in order to promote settlements, rather than the converse.

In addition to the fairly precise and explicit effects of Israeli settlement discussed so far, there is a broader political consequence which impinges on the future of the Palestinian inhabitants as a whole and has serious implications for the peace process itself. For settlement has in fact created in the settlers vested interests which they may not wholly share with any of the other involved parties. As noted in Chapter 1 above, a primary purpose of the law of belligerent occupation is to prevent the creation of vested interests that might hinder the ultimate resolution of the conflict. It has never been difficult to foresee such a result from the establishment of Israeli settlements, particularly in view of the religious justifications advanced for refusing to dismantle settlements once established. When the Ashkenazi Chief Rabbi, General Shlomo Goren, ruled that

Jews are forbidden to transfer to non-Jews any part of the Holy Land,[71] or when Rabbi Levinger, the leader of the Gush Emunim settlers, declared that Palestinian autonomy is a concept forced on Israel by 'goyim who believe we have to give back to the Arabs what has been ours throughout history',[72] each struck a chord of politico-religious enthusiasm whose resonance would undoubtedly have been much diminished had no Israeli settlers been allowed to establish themselves in the occupied territories to begin with.

As it is, the settlers have consolidated their presence to the point where they may even represent a challenge to the authority of the Israeli government itself. An aide to Prime Minister Begin commented during the controversy stirred by the Elon Moreh case that

> Elon Moreh is more than a crisis for the Prime Minister...He's afraid of the possibility of armed resistance by the *Gush Emunim*. He fears it could start a civil war.[73]

Thus, the spectre is raised of an Israeli government so intimidated by the threat of a settler revolt that it feels forced to appease settler demands even against unequivocal and legally justified opposition from the indigenous Palestinians whose interests Israel is legally obliged to protect. Indeed, the Elon Moreh judgement demonstrates that, although rigorously constrained by the law of belligerent occupation, the Israeli government nevertheless yielded to illegality in the face of even less severe domestic political pressure. To accord that government unfettered authority, as the Israeli autonomy proposals would do, could hardly be expected against such a background to result in greater observance of international legality on Israel's part or on the part of the settlers. The presence of settlements in the occupied territories therefore has both presently and prospectively a profoundly destabilizing political impact.

Finally, the settlements' absorption of land, the West Bank's greatest natural asset, must not be overlooked. Because Palestinian villages tend to be tight-knit conglomerations of small buildings,[74] surrounded by extensive agricultural lands[75] sometimes running miles from the village itself, economic displacement of the indigenous Palestinian population can be produced by seizure of such agricultural land without in every case confiscation of the village proper. The available, though undifferentiated, statistics on settlement land are therefore so much the more ominous. By late 1977, Jewish settlement on the West Bank (excluding over 77,000 dunums seized for settlement in East Jerusalem) had removed from potential Arab control approximately 123,000 dunums, equivalent to more than 6% of the area's cultivated land.[76] A more recent Gush Emunim demand for allocation of a further 50,000 acres (200,000 dunums) for settlement[77] would raise the percentage of land controlled by settlers to the equivalent of 16% of the West Bank's total cultivated land.[78] The U.N. Security Council investigative Commission referred to above provided information tending to indicate that 1,480,000 dunums had been seized by the Israeli authorities, 27% of the West Bank's total land area or the equivalent of 74% of its total cultivated land.[79] Whatever the respective shares of cultivated and uncultivated land within these figures, it is clear that a significant proportion of the West Bank's potential assets had already come under Israeli disposition even as the tempo of settlement began to accelerate.

In view of the broadly adverse impact of settlements revealed in the preceding pages it cannot any longer be plausibly argued that the character of the occupied territories remains, as international law demands, unchanged and undisturbed.

Jerusalem

It should be noted at this point that, although Shamgar and other defenders of Israel's measures in the territories occupied in 1967 would not say so, as a matter of law the arguments against Israel's occupation policies apply with equal force to Israeli actions in East Jerusalem where Israel's largest scale settlement activity has been concentrated.[80] As Dr Gerson has rightly indicated in his recent book on Israeli occupation in the West Bank,

> No valid distinction appears to exist between the legitimacy of Israeli claims to sovereignty over the West Bank and those made in regard to East Jerusalem. Both stand or fall on the same merits...It has been the thesis of this work that Israel's legitimate stake in the West Bank is limited to belligerent or, at best, trustee occupation...[81]

Consequently, Israel may no more establish settlements in East

Jerusalem than in other parts of the West Bank, and the attempt in the Plan's autonomy proposals to exclude East Jerusalem from the negotiations on Palestinian rights finds no support in international law.

Conclusion

In summary, then, the law of belligerent occupation provides Israel with no basis for the establishment of permanent civilian settlements in occupied territory, and Israel must seek elsewhere for the means of legitimizing her settlement activities.

2 *Effect of the Plan on the Legality of Settlement*

This conclusion suggests that the taint of illegality on all Israeli settlement activity in occupied territory may be removed only by terminating applicability of the law of belligerent occupation. The point has not been lost on the Gush Emunim settlers: immediately after the Elon Moreh decision was handed down by the High Court of Justice, Gush Emunim called upon the Israeli government to 'change the legal status' of the West Bank so that the area would be subject to Israeli domestic law rather than international law.[82] The following five ways to change an occupied territory's legal status have been recognized in classical international law:

> the area may be set free by the forces of the legitimate sovereign or of his allies; it may be liberated by a successful uprising of the indigenous population; it may be returned to the control of the legitimate sovereign under the terms of a peace treaty; it may be annexed by the occupant under the provisions of such a treaty; and, lastly, it may be annexed by the occupant after the subjugation of the legitimate sovereign.[83]

Although prohibitions and restrictions to be discussed below on the use of force probably make the last possibility obsolete and no longer sanctioned under international law, it is nevertheless helpful to consider the Israeli occupation in the light of these five alternatives.

The Israeli autonomy Plan clearly envisages neither liberation of the territories by the Palestinians or their allies nor a successful uprising by the local populace. In view of the repeatedly declared intention of Prime Minister Begin to prevent the establishment of a foreign government in the occupied territories,[84] the Plan cannot aim at the peaceful handing over of the territories to their legitimate sovereign.

Subjugation, even if permitted under current international law, could not properly be said to have taken place in view of the continued functioning of the Jordanian state and the continued activity in the field of Palestinian guerrilla forces.[85]

There remains the possibility of terminating the state of belligerent occupation by Israeli annexation pursuant to a treaty. And yet, although this would be the only lawful alternative left to Israel to end the application of the laws of belligerent occupation and permit legitimization of settlements, the original Begin Plan did not in fact explicitly propose recognition of Israeli annexation. What is to be made of this seeming anomaly?

Once again demographics may have been a main Israeli concern. Comment on the original Begin Plan revealed the anxiety of some (notable among them former Foreign Minister Abba Eban) lest even the very restrictive provisions in Article 15 for Palestinian acquisition of Israeli citizenship might in time deprive Israel of its Jewish quality.[86] This particular fear may be unduly exaggerated in view of Article 15's very explicit conditioning of Palestinian acquisition of Israeli citizenship on its being 'in accordance with the citizenship law of the state' – thus leaving entirely to Israel the promulgation of any legal restrictions or limitations thought necessary to minimize the effect of Article 15. The general concern, however, remains well founded. Students of Israel's demographic balance have concluded that near the end of this century Israel and the occupied territories combined will probably have an Arab majority so that

> With a majority of its voters non-Jews, a democratic Israel obviously could not function as a Jewish state.[87]

In other words, around the year 2000 a democratic secular Palestine may be coming into existence merely through continuance of present population trends (assuming no great increase in immigration of Russian Jews). Faced with 'a demographic crisis so acute that room to manouevre is virtually nonexistent',[88] Israeli planners had to find a way to avoid democratic assimilation of the occupied territories' inhabitants into the Israeli political system while at the same time maximising Israeli supremacy over those territories. In crude terms, Israel had to manage to have the land but not the people.

The original Begin Plan seemed designed to provide a structure whereby this goal could be achieved. For, coupled with the Begin Plan's security provisions and its granting to *all* the residents of the areas without distinction of citizenship the right to vote for, and serve on, the Administrative Council controlling Arab affairs,[89] Article 20, by purporting to legitimize the residency of a growing Israeli settler population, would have provided the legal basis for increasing Israeli political power in the occupied territories without creating the conditions for any reciprocal influence by Palestinians in Israeli political life.

Furthermore, Article 26 of the Begin Plan provided: 'These principles will be subject to review after a five year period'. That provision would, on the one hand, have allowed the Israeli government to seek revision of the Plan's arrangements to take account of the greater Israeli presence legitimized by Article 20. On the other hand, it would have prevented the Palestinians from implementing changes disadvantageous to Israel, since failure to agree on modifications would presumably have left the *status quo* intact. In any case, the review, unlike negotiations on the Begin Plan itself, would, by virtue of Article 20's legitimizing effect, proceed on the premise that Israeli settlement did not violate international law. In the context of Article 26, Article 20 would appear to have laid much of the basis on which Israel could in the future foreclose the question of sovereignty and could convert the *de facto* territorial supremacy implicit in the Begin Plan into *de jure* supremacy.

And yet, by avoiding an explicit linkage between the Begin Plan and establishment of Israeli sovereignty, Article 26 would have avoided the imputation that Article 20 was an integral part of a larger design to promote Israeli annexation of the occupied territories. This may have been thought to have had legal signifi-cance in light of the opinion of some writers that systematic settlement which displaces indigenous inhabitants is illegal where 'generally evidencing a clear intent to annex the territory'.[90]

Thus the original Begin Plan went as far as Israel probably could go in solving the problem of the occupied territories short of attempting an explicit unilateral annexation which would be forbidden by international law.

B ANNEXATION

Nevertheless, Israel's fundamental legal difficulty remains: settlement cannot be legitimized without a treaty; and a treaty is unlikely to be secured without Israel's abandonment of settlement. The nature of the problem indicates the possible solutions. Israel may persist, though with little hope of success, in efforts to secure a treaty recognizing the *faits accomplis* brought about in the occupied territories through Israel's reliance on its predominant military power there, or it may directly employ the force at its command to effect unilateral annexation regardless of the international legal consequences, as was done in East Jerusalem in June 1967.[91]

As noted above, the latter alternative, in the form of application of Israeli domestic law to the occupied territories, was advocated by Gush Emunim leaders in the wake of the Elon Moreh decision. Israeli Minister of Education Zevulun Hammer appeared to respond to this proposal when he declared that Israel had to find means to legalize settlement without violating Israel's agreement in the Camp David accords to introduce self-rule in the occupied territories.[92] Israeli legal experts had earlier been reported to believe that direct annexation would be impossible because of Israel's commitments under those accords.[93] When right-wing members of the Knesset nevertheless (or, perhaps, consequently) moved that Israeli law be applied in the West Bank and Gaza, the motion was defeated after Prime Minister Begin declared that it would go against the Egyptian-Israeli Peace Treaty of March 1979. Mr Begin significantly qualified this declaration, however, by stating that the extension of Israeli law to the West Bank would not take place so long as negotiations with Egypt continued.[94]

It is interesting to note that annexation was debated in the context of extending the operation of Israeli law to the occupied territories. This recalls the procedure whereby East Jerusalem was annexed in 1967. This is significant, for although Israel's extension of jurisdiction in 1967 was such as to give Israel full national authority in East Jerusalem, it was selective enough to avoid granting full citizenship rights to the Palestinian majority in East Jerusalem. In particular, the Palestinians of East Jerusalem were not given the right to vote in national elections for the Knesset. Extension of jurisdiction may thus be attractive in the larger context as a means of lessening the effects of the ever-present demographic problem discussed earlier.

For the moment, however, the position seemed to be that the Israeli government wished to use the device of direct unilateral annexation as a last resort if Egypt would not be brought to accept the Israeli autonomy plan by agreement. Nevertheless, a basis for the legal rationale of such a unilateral step was already being laid in the statements of Hammer and Begin: namely, that Israel labours under no restriction of international law in this matter but is bound merely by some undertaking to Egypt which would, by implication, be dissolved if Egypt were not forthcoming in the negotiations looking to adoption of the Israeli autonomy scheme.

By this time, however, the Begin Plan itself had undergone a major modification. In May 1979 the Israeli Cabinet approved an addition to the original plan providing that at the end of the five-year interim period Israel would claim sovereignty over the West Bank and the Gaza Strip.[95] Foreign Minister Dayan was reported at that time to have opposed the modified Plan[96] and he later confirmed his having voted against it,[97] His resignation in October, 1979 was explained as in part reflecting his desire that agreement with the Arabs be achieved 'without imposing our sovereignty on them'.[98] In particular, he rejected that annexation of the West Bank and Gaza which he understood the amended autonomy Plan to propose.[99]

The Israeli government's design that autonomy lead to ultimate Israeli annexation had at last become explicit, and it was this purpose that Egypt was asked to accept in the autonomy negotiations on pain of unilateral Israeli action if Egypt refused.

The question of settlements, already linked to the issue of annexation, had thus then been subsumed by that issue both legally and politically.

Given the illegality of unilateral annexation and settlement, it must therefore be the Israeli case that the legal defects in her settlement policy may be cured by an international agreement embodying those aspects of the Plan which envisage Israel's full sovereignty over the occupied territories. In turn, since, in the face of prior sovereignty having legally resided elsewhere, Israel's claim of sovereignty derives its legal effect solely from the fact of Israel's forcible seizure of the territories in 1967 and her continued application of force in them thereafter, it must be legally possible for such an agreement to legitimize the results of Israel's use of force. Whether and to what extent this may be done must now be considered.

C   *AUTONOMY AND THE USE OF FORCE*

Central to the issue of the limits on the use of force is Article 2(4) of the United Nations Charter which provides:

> All Members [of the United Nations] shall refrain in their international relations from the threat or use of force against the territorial integrity or political independence of any State, or in any other manner inconsistent with the Purposes of the United Nations.

It is sometimes argued that this prohibition on the use of force, when read in conjunction with Article 51 of the Charter (discussed below), should not be understood to forbid the use of force in self-defence pending action by the Security Council.[100] Hence, it is said, the adverse consequences of violating Article 2(4) must be taken to apply only to an unlawful use of force, beyond self-defence. Israel's advocates, however, go further and seem to suggest that the lawful use of force should not be merely exculpatory but should actually garner for the militant state benefits to which she would have had no legal entitlement had she not used force.

The Israeli case based on this argument has been summarized by Major-General Chaim Herzog, former Military Governor of the West Bank and Israeli Ambassador to the United Nations, in these words:

> ...[In] 'defensive conquests'...a state may lawfully seize and occupy foreign territory if 'necessary to its self-defense'...a state may require, before it withdraws from territory occupied in a defensive conquest, that satisfactory security arrangements be established to safeguard its security...the state that holds territory through lawful defensive conquest has, vis-à-vis the prior occupant that acquired the territory through unlawful offensive conquest, better title to the land.[101]

This argument could have major significance for implementation of the Israeli autonomy Plan under the terms of an international treaty, if such a treaty purported to legitimize both Israel's annexation of the territories by right of 'better title' and her establishment of settlements there pursuant to her new territorial sovereignty. In that situation the 'defensive conquest' argument could be used to remove the taint from that treaty that it was procured, in violation of customary international law embodied in Article 52 of the Vienna Convention on the Law of Treaties, by such threat or use of force as is prohibited in Article 2(4) of the Charter.[102]

Accepting *arguendo* such sweeping consequences for the lawful/unlawful distinction, one sees that the applicability of Article 51 of the Charter to the situation produced by the entry of Israeli forces into the occupied territories is important not only for the legal status of the Israeli presence – and that presence's manifestations – in the areas but also for the legality of a treaty embodying the autonomy Plan.

Putting aside questions about the legality of Israel's initiating the use of force against Egypt in 1967[103] and about Jordan's claim to have subsequently opened fire on Israeli positions in collective self-defence with Egypt in accordance with Article 51, and assuming for the sake of argument the position most favourable to Israel on these questions, one may proceed to the central issue. Is Israel entitled by reason of Article 51 to claim by virtue of self-defence to have acquired 'better title', and hence sovereign rights, over the occupied territories and to be thus enabled legitimately to establish permanent civilian settlements there?

The relevant language of Article 51 is:

Nothing in the present Charter shall impair the inherent right of individual or collective self-defense if an armed attack occurs against a Member of the United Nations, until the Security Council has taken the measures necessary to maintain international peace and security.

The right of self-defence thus recognized does not give *carte blanche* for the use of force. Rather, the sole legitimate objective for self-defence is that stated in clear and emphatic language by Bowett in his authoritative treatise on the subject:

self-defence operates to protect essential rights from irreparable harm in circumstances in which alternative means of protection are unavailable; its function is to preserve or restore the legal *status quo*, and not to take on a remedial or repressive character in order to enforce legal rights.[104]

When self-defence has removed the immediate danger which provoked it, it has served its purpose of restoring the defending state to the position of safety it was in before the particular use of force at issue became necessary. Self-defence thereupon loses its power to justify continued use of force by the formerly defending state, even when that state might have other grievances that can be redressed by further reliance on force.

This close connection between the immediacy of the danger to be met and the limits to be imposed on the use of force has been recognized in international law at least since United States Secretary of State Webster, in his 1842 Note in the *Caroline Case*, wrote:

> It will be for [the defending state] to show...that...even supposing the necessity of the moment authorized [it] to [act with force], [it] did nothing unreasonable or excessive; since the act justified by the necessity of self-defense, must be limited by that necessity, and kept clearly within it.[105]

Israeli Ambassador Herzog, when defending Israel's raid on Entebbe in 1976, acknowledged Webster's statement as 'the classic formulation' of the 'right of self-defense... enshrined in international law and the Charter of the United Nations'.[106]

It is evident both that Israel's purported immediate need to defend itself in 1967 can hardly have its effects so prolonged as to justify annexation of the occupied territories in 1985 or 1986 and that a return to the *status quo* as it was at the outbreak of the 1967 war would not leave Israel with sovereignty over the occupied territories or permit continuance of any Israeli civilian settlements. Use of force to accomplish such changes in the *status quo* therefore cannot be excused by reliance on the doctrine of self-defence.

Nevertheless, Israel has consistently since 1967 specifically rejected a complete return to the pre-war *status quo*. Prime Minister Begin declared, even after the signing of the 1979 Egyptian-Israeli Peace Treaty that 'There will never again be a border in the western part of the Land of Israel'.[107] Israel's refusal to go back to the *status quo* has been most evident in discussions on implementation of United Nations Security Council Resolution 242 (examined further below). Mr Begin has indicated that the principles of Resolution 242 are compatible with Israel's rejection of a Palestinian state 'in Eretz-Israel' and with her rejection of a return to the 1967 borders.[108] He has further declared that there is no contradiction between the 1977 Begin Plan and the Resolution (as thus understood).[109]

Hence, when Bowett states that self-defence cannot be used as a justification for 'remedial' or 'repressive' measures he highlights another area of concern over Israel's use of force in establishing and maintaining her current occupation. For it is beyond doubt that Israel uses 'defensive conquest' to justify altering the pre-war *status quo* in her favour, not merely by the establishment of settlements but also by the manipulation of occupation as a bargaining counter in efforts to achieve Israel's long-term political goals. Such manipulation is implicit in Herzog's statement on 'defensive conquest' quoted above, and it is explicit in the following excerpt from the same speech:

> The Arab states must learn that they will not be able to change the legal status, the geographical nature and the demographic composition of the territories by pushing through yet another anti-Israel resolution at the United Nations. They will only be able to obtain changes by fulfilling Resolution 242 and negotiating secure and recognized boundaries with Israel.[110]

Given that it is Israel that contemplates changing the legal status and demographic composition of the territories and has already set about doing so, Herzog must be understood to mean that the Arab states will be unable even to maintain the 1967 *status quo* unless they 'fulfill' Resolution 242. In view, however, of Prime Minister Begin's explication of that Resolution, Herzog's statement signifies that any effort by the United Nations to restore legality to the occupied territories by terminating Israel's occupation or ending Israeli settlement will be frustrated by Israel's reliance on her use of force to dominate those areas, and it indicates further that the Arab states will be unable to vindicate the international legal rights of the Palestinians in occupied territory unless those states agree, contrary to the wishes of the Palestinians, to recognize some Israeli acquisition of territory by force with the concomitant Israeli settlements.

Clearly, 'defensive conquest' has so far departed from restoring the *status quo* that Israel now wishes to use it to destroy the *status quo* by holding the occupied territories hostage against Arab recognition of Israel's illegal acts. This extraordinary perversion of the legal doctrine recalls the statement of one scholar that

> it would be a curious law of self-defence that permitted the defender in the course of his defence to seize and keep the resources and territory of the attacker.[111]

Just how curious is emphasized by further consideration of Article 51 which, as indicated above, permits self-defence 'until the Security Council has taken the measures necessary to maintain international peace and security'. There can be no doubt that, as Brierly says, 'any exercise of the right of self defence is expressly made subject to the judgement and control of the [Security] Council'.[112] Consequently a state acting first as it sees fit may do so 'at its own peril and...subject to scrutiny by the Security Council'.[113] For this reason, then, the Security Council may impose what limitations it considers appropriate in each case regardless of the initial lawfulness or unlawfulness of the original use of force.[114]

In Security Council Resolution 242 the Council did in fact speak in the aftermath of the 1967 war and Israel's occupation of Arab territory,[115] although advocates of the Israeli position for long disputed the binding character of the Resolution. This defect may be taken to have been cured by Resolution 338[116] of October 22, 1973 which did bind the parties to apply Resolution 242.

Resolution 242 first emphasizes 'the inadmissibility of the acquisition of territory by *war*'[117] (emphasis supplied). One writer suggests in effect that the use of the word 'war' is meant to apply to Israel's preemptive use of force in 1967 without labelling Israel the aggressor.[118] If this is a correct interpretation (and that may be granted for the sake of argument, since it would appear the reading most favourable to Israel), the Resolution would mean that, even when a non-aggressor – *ipso facto* a user of force in self-defence – employs force, he cannot by that employment alone acquire valid title over territory conquered in the course of defence. The Resolution's 'withdrawal clause', calling for 'Withdrawal of Israel armed forces from territories occupied in the recent conflict',[119] may then be understood to apply this general rule to the specific situation faced after the 1967 war. As an application of the clearly-enunciated general rule, the withdrawal clause's vagueness in particularizing the territories from which Israel is to withdraw cannot compel the conclusion that the clause was meant to authorize Israeli annexation of part of the territories. Such a conclusion would in any case lead to the logical inconsistency of the Resolution's condoning in the withdrawal clause what the preamble's governing principle holds inadmissible.

The conclusion then must be that Israeli acquisition of territory and her settlements therein as a result, and by means, of her use of force in 1967 are impermissible. Israel derived no 'better title' (indeed no title at all) from acting in self-defence and she acquired no sovereign rights over the occupied territories such as would free her from her obligations under the laws of belligerent occupation. Hence, Israel possesses no right to regard the territories as subject to her acquisition failing an accommodation by the Arab states or the Palestinians. It may even be impermissible for Israel to hold the territories in lieu of peace as a kind of prospective self-defence against possible future action by the Arab states or the Palestinians to vindicate Palestinian rights.[120]

Consequently, insofar as Israel, pursuant to her military seizure of the occupied territories in 1967, implements a policy of annexation or establishes settlements she is engaging in an illegal use of force. Without that illegality there could have been no settlement in the occupied territories, and it follows that a treaty aiming to legitimize such settlements could only be procured in conseqence of that illegal use of force.

Furthermore, it must be recalled that the peaceful settlement of disputes in conformity with the principles of justice and international law is a fundamental duty imposed on United Nations' members by the Charter.[121] Settlement of disputes by peaceful means is the only legitimate method permitted an individual state for resolution of its international conflicts when the justification of self-defence is unavailable to exculpate the use of force.[122] A threat or use of force in disregard of this duty would thus be a reliance on force 'inconsistent with the Purposes of the United Nations' within the meaning of Article 2(4) of the Charter. Israel is therefore obliged to work for a peaceful solution of the Palestinian problem, and there is no legal justification for Israel to spurn her duty to make peace merely because certain situations created by Israel's illegal use of force, such as civilian settlements, are rejected by the Palestinians or other Arab states. Consequently, to the extent that Israel nevertheless utilizes the deliberately produced practical and psychological effects of her illegal use of force in the occupied territories to extort from the Arabs, under threat of an Israeli refusal otherwise to conclude peace, a treaty accepting Israeli annexation or settlement, that treaty will have been procured in consequence of an illegal use of force in violation of the United Nations Charter.

What are the implications of these conclusions for attempts by treaty to legitimize Israeli annexation or civilian settlements?

D   ATTEMPTED LEGITIMATION

In his 1953 Report to the International Law Commission, Sir Hersch Lauterpacht, as Special Rapporteur on the law of treaties, observed that

> in so far as war or force or threats of force constitute an internationally illegal act, the results of the illegality – namely, a treaty imposed in connection with or in consequence thereof – are governed by the principle that an illegal act cannot produce legal rights for the benefit of the law-breaker.[123]

Furthermore, Article 103 of the United Nations Charter, in subordinating all other treaty obligations to those in the Charter, effectively renders all other agreements void and unenforceable to the extent of their inconsistency with the Charter.[124] The principle has been reflected in Article 52 of the Vienna Convention on the Law of Treaties[125] which states:

> A treaty is void if its conclusion has been procured by the threat or use of force in violation of the principles of international law embodied in the Charter of the United Nations.

In presenting its draft of this article, the International Law Commission explained the principle and effect of considering a treaty so procured to be void:

> a treaty procured by a threat or use of force in violation of the principles of the Charter must be characterised as void, rather than as voidable at the instance of the injured party. Even if it were conceivable that after being liberated from the influence of a threat or of a use of force a state might wish to allow a treaty procured from it by such means, the Commission considered it essential that the treaty should be regarded in law as void *ab initio*. This would enable the state concerned to take its decision in regard to the maintenance of the treaty in a position of full legal equality with the other state. If, therefore, the treaty were maintained in force, it would in effect be by the conclusion of a new treaty and not by the recognition of the validity of a treaty procured by means contrary to the most fundamental principles of the Charter of the United Nations.[126]

This reasoning is equally as applicable to the rule of customary international law as to the formulation of that rule in Article 52 of the Vienna Convention.

Viewing in this light a treaty incorporating the Israeli autonomy Plan and based on illegal Israeli use of force as discussed in Section C above, one immediately sees that such a treaty would be void from the beginning and without any legal effect. That treaty could not bestow legality on the Israeli autonomy Plan and could not legitimate Israeli annexation or settlements.

Because of the doctrine of non-recognition to be discussed below, this conclusion has considerable significance for the peace process itself and for the broader issue of Palestinian rights.

For it has over many decades been an acknowledged principle of international law, usually called the Stimson Doctrine but in fact predating that 1932 formulation, that states may refuse to recognize 'any territorial arrangement that is not obtained by pacific means'.[127] But Brownlie has very persuasively argued that this doctrine of non-recognition has developed so as to lose its discretionary character and to have become obligatory. Aside from acknowledgement of such a duty in various international agreements,[128] Brownlie sees the principle generally accepted and applied in state practice before and during World War II[129] in the context of progressive restriction of the scope for permissible use of force.[130] He concludes that

the essential criminality of wars of aggression and analogous forms of the use of force as an instrument of national policy has altered the nature of recognition in such circumstances and given it the character of complicity in criminal activity.[131]

Precisely what may be uses of force analogous to wars of aggression has been delineated in the U.N. General Assembly's 1974 Resolution on the Definition of Aggression[132] which, in Article 3(a), qualifies as an act of aggression

any annexation by the use of force of the territory of another State or part thereof.

Indeed, Brownlie suggests that mere 'recognition of annexation would be...a violation of the sovereignty of the state which was a victim of the use or threat of force'.[133]

There is thus a good case to be made that, even if Israel could procure from some Arab state a treaty purporting to adopt the Israeli autonomy Plan and thereby to legitimize illegal Israeli annexation and settlement, the international community would be obliged, in order to avoid implicating itself in Israeli illegalities, to refuse recognition to that treaty and its consequences. The Palestinians and their supporters would no doubt go further and urge that there was a duty to take positive action to resist the aggression implicit in such a treaty.

In addition, since 'it is in principle possible to treat *de jure* recognition of an illegal acquisition as revocable at any time',[134] an Arab party to a treaty with Israel void *ab initio* would be legally justified in withdrawing its recognition of the Israeli autonomy arrangements whenever the kaleidoscopic changes of Middle Eastern politics made that seem advisable.

Illegal imposition of Israel's autonomy Plan would thus lay a legal basis for further discord and conflict not only in the Middle East but internationally as well.

The heavy weight of illegality and invalidity that would lie on the autonomy treaty affects also the legal standing of any Arab state that pretends to sign such a treaty on behalf of the Palestinians. President Sadat declared that he would negotiate on the Palestinians' behalf since 'The West Bank and Gaza do not belong to the P.L.O. They belong to us and the rest of the Arab nation'.[135] The discussion above of Palestinian sovereignty has indicated enough of the foundation of Palestinian claims to the occupied territories to show how preposterous President Sadat's assertion is from a legal point of view. But from a practical perspective many might be tempted to accept the Egyptian role of self-appointed representative of the Palestinians if that role were undertaken and acted out in a spirit of good faith and concern for legality. It is submitted that the patent illegality of a treaty embodying the Plan would preclude the presumption of such good faith or concern on Egypt's part if she persisted in working towards such a treaty once the Palestinians' legal objections had been made plain. Indeed, President Sadat is already on notice that a number of West Bank Palestinian leaders believe he is 'unjustifiably interfering' in Palestinian affairs,[136] and his legal standing in the circumstances is at best doubtful.

On many levels, therefore, treaty implementation of the Israeli autonomy Plan would be at the least disrupting and unproductive and at the worst would pull all those involved into a legal and political maelstrom.

If autonomy as envisaged by Israel is likely to prove incapable of resolving the core question of the Middle East problem, and indeed only exacerbate it, does any reasonable alternative squarely based on accepted international law present itself? To answer this properly one must first consider an aspect of the Palestinian issue which the Plan successfully ignored altogether: Palestinian claims to self-determination.

NOTES

1   MERIP REPORTS No. 59 at 22–23 (Middle East Research and Information Project, August 1977).
2   Cf. the views of Prof. Moshe Arens on the connection between settlement and immigration in the Jerusalem Post, Jan. 5, 1979, p.1.
3   Statement by Ambassador Charles W. Yost, July 1, 1969, United States Mission to the United Nations, Press Release USUN–70 (69) *reprinted in* THE ARAB-ISRAELI CONFLICT 1098, 1099 (Moore ed., abr. ed. 1977).
4   *See* Letter of September 22, 1978 from President Carter to Prime Minister Begin reaffirming the American position on Jerusalem, in Camp David package of documents, 78 DEPT. OF STATE BULL. (October, 1978) at 7–9.
5   Letter dated April 21, 1978 from State Department Legal Adviser Hansell to Chairmen Fraser and Hamilton in ISRAELI SETTLEMENTS IN THE OCCUPIED TERRITORIES: HEARINGS BEFORE THE SUB-COMMITTEES ON INTERNATIONAL ORGANIZ-ATIONS AND ON EUROPE AND THE MIDDLE EAST OF THE COMMITTEE ON INTERNATIONAL RELATIONS HOUSE OF REPRESENTATIVES, Ninety Fifth Congress, First Session, September 12, 21; and October 19, 1977; U.S. Government Printing Office, Washington, 1978, pages 167–172. Hereinafter this volume will be cited as HEARINGS.
6   HEARINGS 170.
7   *Id.*, 170–171.
8   *See* on this event R. PFAFF, JERUSALEM: KEYSTONE OF AN ARAB-ISRAELI SETTLEMENT 40–41 (1969); E. WILSON, JERUSALEM KEY TO PEACE 113 (1970); GERSON, ISRAEL, THE WEST BANK AND INTER-NATIONAL LAW 162–163; HEARINGS at 8, 12, 40.
9   Cf. HERZOG, WHO STANDS ACCUSED 88–89, and 92.

10 *See* Y. Blum, *The Missing Reversioner: Reflections on the Status of Judea and Samaria*, 3 Is. L. R. 279 (1968).

11 Shamgar, *The Observance of International Law in the Administered Territories*, in THE ARAB-ISRAELI CONFLICT, *supra* n.3, 489, at 490, 491, 492–493.

12 K. Skubiszewski, *Use of Force by States. Collective Security. Law of War and Neutrality*, in MANUAL OF PUBLIC INTERNATIONAL LAW, ed. M. Sørensen, 739, 833; PICTET, HUMANITARIAN LAW AND THE PROTECTION OF WAR VICTIMS 129 (1975); II LAUTERPACHT-OPPENHEIM 451–452.

13 I.C.R.C. COMMENTARY on the Fourth Geneva Convention 77.

14 S.C. Res. 237, 22 U.N. SCOR Resolutions, U.N. Doc. S/INF/22/Rev. 2 at 5.

15 *Id.*

16 Cf. BROWNLIE, PRINCIPLES OF PUBLIC INTERNATIONAL LAW 512–515 (3rd ed.).

17 I.C.R.C. COMMENTARY 79.

18 Quoted in CATTAN, PALESTINE AND INTERNATIONAL LAW 65.

19 *See* Gerson, *Trustee-Occupant: The Legal Status of Israel's Presence in the West Bank*, 14 HARV. INT'L L.J. 1, 23–24 note 70 quoting El Araby.

20 CATTAN, note 18 *supra*, at 30–32.

21 *Id.*, at 67.

22 *Id.*, at 42.

23 *Id.*, at 81; II LAUTERPACHT-OPPENHEIM 433.

24 CATTAN 82.

25 Gerson, note 19 *supra*.

26 *Id.*, at 28.

27 *Id.*, at 24–27.

28 *Id.*, at 27.

29 *Id.*, at 29–30.

30 Quoted in Gerson, note 19 *supra*, at 29.

31 *Id.*, at 30.

32 *Id.*, at 31.

33 *Id.*, at 33.

34 *Id.*, at 34.

35 *Id.*, at 34–35.

36 *Id.*, at 35.

37 BROWNLIE, note 16 *supra*, at xxxviii.
38 Gerson, note 19 *supra*, at 40 and 43.
39 *Id.*
40 CATTAN, note 18 *supra*, at 142–146.
41 Gerson, note 19 *supra*, at 39.
42 *Id.*, at 40.
43 I.C.R.C. COMMENTARY, note 13 *supra*, at 73.
44 *Id.*, at 72–80.
45 N.Y. Times, Feb. 17, 1978, at A2, col.3.
46 N.Y. Times, July 15, 1979, at 7, col.1; XVI UN CHRONICLE, No. 6, at 15 (July-October, 1979).
47 Christian Science Monitor, Sept. 13, 1979, p.1.
48 *Id.*
49 N.Y. Times, Nov. 12 1979, p.A3, cols. 3–6.
50 Boston Globe, Nov. 16, 1979, p.3.
51 Quoted in MERIP REPORTS No. 59, note 1 *supra*, at 19.
52 *Id.*, at 22.
53 *Id.*, at 22–23.
54 M. Drobles, *Master Plan for the Development of Judea and Samaria 1979–1983* (Jerusalem, October, 1978) in Section I, in unofficial English translation.
55 Wall Street Journal, July 25, 1979, p.1.
56 Case No. HCJ 390/79, judgement given October 22, 1979. *See* N.Y. Times, Oct. 23, 1979, p.1, cols. 3–4; Boston Globe, Oct. 23, 1979. p.1; Wall Street Journal, Oct. 23, 1979. p.2.; Christian Science Monitor, Oct. 23, 1979. p.3. *and* Oct. 26, 1979, p.9.
57 Unofficial Israeli government Press Bulletin translation dated October 24, 1979, at p.13: 'The political consideration was, therefore, the dominant factor in the Ministerial Defense Committee's decision to establish the settlement at that site...'
58 *Id.*, at 14, quoting an affidavit submitted on behalf of the Gush Emunim settlers.
59 *Id.*, at 20.
60 *Id.*
61 Christian Science Monitor, Oct. 26, 1979, p.1.
62 N.Y. Times, Oct. 29, 1979, p.A3, cols. 1–2.
63 Drobles Plan, note 54 *supra*, Section I.
64 *Id.*
65 Jerusalem Post International Ed., Nov. 18–25, 1979, p.13.

66 *Id.*
67 *Id.*
68 Drobles Plan, note 54 *supra*, Section I.
69 Cf. Boston Globe, Nov. 2, 1979, p.16.
70 The Jerusalem Post, Jan. 5, 1979, p.1, cols. 1–3.
71 N.Y. Times, Aug. 22, 1979, p.A12, cols. 4–5.
72 N.Y. Times, June 25, 1979, p.A2, cols. 3–6.
73 TIME, Nov. 26, 1979, at 69–70.
74 PATAI, THE KINGDOM OF JORDAN 201.
75 *Id.*, at 202.
76 HEARINGS, note 5 *supra*, at 38–42 on seized land. Area of cultivated land in TUMA & DARIN-DRABKIN, THE ECONOMIC CASE FOR PALESTINE 59 (1978).
77 N.Y. Times, Oct. 16, 1979, p.A5, cols. 1–6.
78 *See* TUMA & DARIN-DRABKIN, note 76 *supra*, at 59 where total of cultivated land is given as 2,000 sq. kms., i.e., 2,000,000 dunums.
79 The percentage seized is given in XVI UN CHRONICLE No. 6, at 15 (July–October, 1979). The comparison in the text is based on 27% of 5,500 sq. kms. given as total land area of the West Bank in TUMA & DARIN-DRABKIN, note 76 *supra*, at 52.
80 HEARINGS, note 5 *supra*, at 38–42.
81 GERSON, ISRAEL, THE WEST BANK AND INTER-NATIONAL LAW 214 (1978).
82 Christian Science Monitor, Nov. 15, 1979, p.6; cf. also Christian Science Monitor, Oct. 26, 1979, p.1. *and* N.Y. Times, Oct. 23, 1979, p.1, cols 3–4; Boston Globe, Oct. 23, 1979, p.1.
83 VON GLAHN, LAW AMONG NATIONS 688 (3rd ed.).
84 Reported by Michael Elkins in BBC World Service programme 'From Our Own Correspondents', March 19, 1978.
85 Gerson, note 19 *supra*, at 6–7 and note 16.
86 Jerusalem Post Int'l Ed., Apr. 4, 1978, at 2, col. 3.
87 Breindel & Eberstadt, 'Israel's Numbers Game', N.Y. Times, Aug. 27, 1979, p.A 17, cols. 5–6.
88 *Id.*
89 Begin Plan, Articles 4 & 5.
90 GERSON, note 81 *supra*, at 237.
91 *Id.*, at 211 and 228, note 17. Cf. PFAFF, note 8 *supra*, at 34–40.

92 N.Y. Times, Oct. 29, 1979, p.A3, cols. 1 & 2.

93 N.Y. Times, Oct. 23, 1979, p.A1, cols. 3 & 4.

94 BBC World Service News broadcast, Dec. 26, 1979.

95 N.Y. Times, May 9, 1979, at A11, col. l.

96 N.Y. Times, May 22, 1979, p.1, col. 1.

97 Boston Globe, Oct. 24, 1979, p.15.

98 *Id. Also* N.Y. Times, Oct. 24, 1979, p.A3, cols. 3–6.

99 Boston Globe, Oct. 27, 1979, p.12.

100 Schwebel, *What Weight to Conquest*, in THE ARAB-ISRAELI CONFLICT, note 3 *supra*, at 357, 360.

101 HERZOG, note 9 *supra*, at 90.

102 Cf. GREIG, INTERNATIONAL LAW 161 (2nd ed.).

103 On 'anticipatory self-defence', *see* GREIG, note 102 *supra*, at 892–894. Counter-argument in CATTAN 126–135. The Arab case finds some interesting support in Gerson, note 19 *supra*, at 18–19 quoting Israeli air force chief Ezer Weizman, later Defence Minister in the Begin government, who stated in a 1972 interview:

> We had to attack because the enemy, intentionally or not, brought about a situation in which he tried to force upon us basic political decisions under the threat of military force. Perhaps the Egyptians would never have attacked. Perhaps we would have accepted the minority opinion not to go to war but to transport in the straits via a convoy under a Norwegian or Danish flag. Then we would have accepted second-class statehood; and if the Arabs had attacked first they would have caused us more losses and the victory would have taken longer.

On this reading of the facts, Gerson concludes, 'Egyptian attack would then not have been "imminent"' – imminence usually being held required to justify 'anticipatory self-defence', *see* GREIG at 893.

104 BOWETT, SELF-DEFENCE IN INTERNATIONAL LAW 11.

105 BROWNLIE, INTERNATIONAL LAW AND THE USE OF FORCE BY STATES 43.

106 Quoted in HARRIS, CASES AND MATERIALS ON INTERNATIONAL LAW 684 (2nd ed.).

107 N.Y. Times, May 3, 1979, at A5, col. 1.

108 Jerusalem Post Int'l Ed., June 28, 1977, p.5.

109 N.Y. Times, March 9, 1978, p.1, col. 2.

110 HERZOG, note 9 *supra*, at 98–99.

111 JENNINGS, THE ACQUISITION OF TERRITORY IN INTERNATIONAL LAW 55, quoted in GREIG, note 102 *supra*, at 161.

112 BRIERLY, THE LAW OF NATIONS 416 (6th ed.).

113 VON GLAHN, note 83 *supra*, at 132.

114 *Id.*

115 Sec. Council Res. 242, 22 U.N. SCOR Resolutions, U.N. Doc. S/INF/Rev. 2 at 8–9 (November 22, 1967).

116 Sec. Council Res. 338, 28 U.N. SCOR Resolutions, U.N. Doc. S/INF/29 at 10 (October 22, 1973).

117 Resolution 242, note 115 *supra*.

118 Schwebel, note 100 *supra*, at 357 note 4.

119 Resolution 242, note 115 *supra*, Paragraph 1(i).

120 *See* GREIG, note 102 *supra*, at 896.

121 I LAUTERPACHT-OPPENHEIM 403–406.

122 VON GLAHN, note 83 *supra*, at 456.

123 Lauterpacht quoted in CATTAN, note 18 *supra*, at 155.

124 I LAUTERPACHT-OPPENHEIM 896.

125 Vienna Convention on the Law of Treaties, U.N. Conf. on the Law of Treaties, Documents of the Conference (U.N. Doc. A/CONF. 39/27) at 289.

126 Year Book of the International Law Commission, 1966, II, at 246–247, quoted in HARRIS, note 16 *supra*, at 638.

127 The Anti-War Treaty of 1933, U.S.T.S. No. 906, 163 L.N.T.S. 393, Article II. *See also* I LAUTERPACHT-OPPENHEIM 142–145, suggesting that the principle may already have been obligatory on members of the League of Nations.

128 BROWNLIE, note 105 *supra*, at 410–413.

129 *Id.*, at 413–418.

130 *Id.*, at 418.

131 *Id.*

132 G.A. Res. 3314, 29 U.N. GAOR Supp. 21. (1974).

133 BROWNLIE, note 105 *supra*, at 419.

134 *Id.*, at 421.

135 N.Y. Times, May 3, 1979, p.A5, col. 1.

136 The Jerusalem Post, November 8, 1978, p.3.

5   Self-determination and Palestinian Rights

Self-determination has been defined as 'the right of cohesive national groups ('peoples') to choose for themselves a form of political organization and their relation to other groups'.[1] Although Sir Thomas More, as long ago as 1516, wrote of something akin to self-determination as a principle of rational politics,[2] sharpening of the concept into a legal requirement began with certain declarations of President Woodrow Wilson during World War I. In 1917 Wilson enunciated the rationale of self-determination in these words:

> No peace can last, or ought to last, which does not recognize and accept the principle that governments derive all their just powers from the consent of the governed, and that no right anywhere exists to hand people about from sovereignty to sovereignty as if they were property.[3]

Self-determination gained its first significant recognition as a legal principle[4] in the 1945 Charter of the United Nations where it is indicated to be a basis for 'friendly relations among nations'[5] and for 'peaceful and friendly relations among nations'.[6] This recognition was furthered by the General Assembly's promulgation in 1966 of the 'Human Rights Covenants' which specifically acknowledge the 'right of self-determination' in their identical first articles.[7] Most important as an expression of United Nations practice,[8] and possessing law-making effect,[9] was the General Assembly's 1960 Declaration on the Granting of Independence

101

to Colonial Countries and Peoples.[10] The Declaration is in the form of an authoritative interpretation of the Charter which makes respect for the principle of self-determination a Charter obligation, not merely an exhortation.[11] After examining these and other references in United Nations resolutions and elsewhere, Brownlie concludes that 'the practice of United Nations organs has established the principle as a part of the law of the United Nations'.[12] Confirmation of this conclusion is to be found in the International Court of Justice's Advisory Opinion in the *Western Sahara Case* where Judge Dillard in his concurring separate opinion determined that the 'pronouncements of the Court thus indicate ... that a norm of international law has emerged' applying the principle of self-determination to non-self-governing territories which are under the aegis of the United Nations.[13] One may agree with Brownlie, therefore, that self-determination now 'is a legal principle'.[14]

Indeed, Brownlie is prepared to go further and suggest that self-determination was at least in the process of becoming, and may already have become, a principle of the *jus cogens,*[15] i.e. the fundamental rules of customary international law which cannot be set aside by mere treaty or acquiescence.[16] Rights under *jus cogens* are consequently said to be 'inherent' and 'inalienable'.[17]

A recent study of the Palestinians' right of self-determination, published under the auspices of the United Nations,[18] traces the affirmation of that right in a series of General Assembly resolutions beginning in 1970.[19] It is not necessary here to examine the progression of those resolutions in detail, but several important points deserve notice.

The resolutions recognize a broad group of Palestinian 'inalienable rights', indicating thereby that the relevant Palestinian rights derive from the *jus cogens* and are consequently indelible and not legally subject to diminution or abandonment even by a treaty. Within that category of 'inalienable rights' the resolutions reaffirm specifically the right of self-determination without external interference and also the right to national independence and sovereignty. Such reaffirmation was latterly accompanied by a recognition that the Palestinian people is a principal party in the establishment of a just and lasting peace in the area.[20] The effect of the resolutions is thus in general to co-ordinate the position of the international community with that of the 1974 Rabat Conference of Arab heads of state in confirming the centrality of the Palestinians in any comprehensive Middle East peace and their right to participate directly in the settlement of their own future. In implementation of these conclusions the General Assembly has accepted the Rabat Conference's designation of the Palestine Liberation Organization as the sole legitimate representative of the Palestinian people.[21]

For the Palestinians confirmation of their right of self-determination brings in its train important legal consequences. These may be deduced from Brownlie's observation that

> the principle [of self-determination] appears to have corollaries which may include the following: ... (2) the principle may compensate for a partial lack of certain *desiderata* in the fields of statehood and recognition; ... (4) territory inhabited by peoples not organized as a state cannot be regarded as *terra nullius* susceptible to appropriation by individual states in case of abandonment by the existing sovereign.[22]

Brownlie's corollary number (2) refers in part to the self-determination principle's being 'set against the concept of effective government' as a qualification of statehood,[23] and he goes on: 'The relevant question may now be: in whose interest and for what legal purpose is government "effective"?'.[24] One may infer from this that an administration which attempts to implement the desire of its people for independent statehood may rely on the principle of self-determination to overcome objections that the administration is unable to exert complete control over the national territory in the face of the use of force by a non-representative government. The refusal of such a non-representative government, or of its allies, to accept the new state would not then act as a legal impediment to recognition of the new administration by the international community as a whole, particularly if self-determination is accepted as a norm of *jus cogens*. Similar considerations would apply in the case of a government-in-exile whose

> legal status ... is consequential on the legal condition of the community it claims to represent, which may be a state, belligerent community, or non-self-governing people. *Prima facie* its legal status will be established the more readily when its exclusion from the community of which it is an agency results from acts contrary to the *jus cogens*, for example, an unlawful resort to force.[25]

It is evident that this corollary of the right of self-determination would be of prime importance if a structure of Palestinian autonomy were established, either according to the Israeli Plan or to some other. For an Administrative Council (to use the Begin Plan's concept) which would be composed largely of Palestinians could attempt at some point to claim international status by relying on self-determination to 'compensate', in Professor Brownlie's word, for some of the missing *desiderata* of statehood. After the publication of the Begin Plan in 1977, Israeli commentators were quick to note the possibilities for such an autonomous expansion of the Begin Plan's 'autonomy',[26] but Mr Begin later responded characteristically to such concerns by pledging to his Herut Party supporters that all members of the Administrative Council would be instantly arrested if they dared proclaim an independent Palestinian state.[27] Press analysis suggested that Israeli insistence that the Administrative Council should derive its authority solely from the Israeli military government was also intended to deny the Council any constitutional basis for seizing independence.[28] In the light of Brownlie's corollary, however, such preventive or counter measures would appear legally ineffective against a legitimate attempt to exercise a right of self-determination. Indeed, such measures could in some circumstances enhance the claims of an administration or exile government whose inability to function fully and effectively on its own territory resulted from the use of force against it. A representative Palestinian body would not need to base the legitimacy of its existence on Israeli devolution of powers and Israeli hostility towards it would not undermine that legitimacy.

This point is emphasized by Brownlie's corollary number (4), which implies that the principle of self-determination precludes considering a territory as without a sovereign (and hence *terra nullius* capable of acquisition) merely because its inhabitants have not yet been able to establish themselves as an independent state. We have seen above that Dr Allan Gerson concluded in his studies of the Israeli occupation of Palestinian territories that those territories were not *res* or *terra nullius* because the international community, through the League of Nations and the United Nations, had expressly recognized latent Palestinian sovereignty over them. Palestinian rights, in that analysis, would then depend on recognition by the international community. Self-determination, however, is a more fundamental right based on the nature of the international community in the twentieth century and the primary principles which are necessary for its continued existence and functioning within the framework of the United Nations Charter. The right of Palestinians to effectuate their sovereignty therefore persists because of its concordance with that fundamental principle and not because of Israeli or international recognition of that right.

Thus, the position with respect to autonomy is not that Israel gives or withdraws Palestinian self-determination at will but that Israel may merely acknowledge, or rescind acknowledgement of, the Palestinians' exercise of their rights. Therefore, genuine expressions of Palestinian national aspirations by means of machinery instituted by Israel for her own purposes is not invalidated by subsequent Israeli interference with that machinery.

Central to the concept of self-determination is the requirement that it be exercized by a population which constitutes a 'people'.[29] It is not surprising that Israeli analysts have attempted to undermine support for Palestinian self-determination by denying the Palestinians the status of a people.[30] The argument is rejected by the Palestinians who point to their long-term common linguistic, ethnic, social and (till 1948) geographical attachment to their land. The view that the Palestinian Arabs are a national group has a long history[31] and seemingly has such interesting contemporary proponents as former Israeli Foreign Minister Eban and Minister of Defence Ezer Weizman.[32] In any event, one may think that the Israeli argument comes strangely from representatives of a country that has, in the face of all criteria to the contrary, asserted its nationhood on the basis of a multilingual population gathered in from the four corners of the world after a 2000-year separation from their 'homeland'.[33]

Nevertheless, the issue of the Palestinians' status as a people remains a central (if not always acknowledged) issue in the debate on autonomy, and its importance explains much of the development of that debate since the publication of the Begin Plan in December 1977. For, as may be inferred from the previous discussion, recognition of the status necessarily entails acceptance of the rights pertaining to that status. To acknowledge that the Palestinians, as a people, are an embryonic member of the international community is implicitly to agree that they are entitled to the rights of such a member.

Thus, it would appear to have been by design that, in the first declaration of its kind by the United States, the Soviet-American

Statement on the Middle East of October 1, 1977[34] linked status and rights in calling for resolution of all questions in the area 'including insuring the legitimate rights of the Palestinian people'. This language was welcomed by the Palestine Liberation Organization as a considerable advance towards recognition of Palestinian claims.[35] The importance of the clause seemed also not to have been lost on Israeli Finance Minister Ehrlich who indicated that in the view of the Statement Israel faced an 'emergency period'.[36] And yet, while United Nations resolutions regularly speak of 'inalienable' rights, the Statement rather classified them as 'legitimate'. The attempted distinction may have been more significant than was originally perceived.

Putting aside the semantic questions of whether 'rights', if genuine, could be anything other than 'legitimate' and whether there could legally be 'illegitimate' rights, one may consider why the Statement failed to use the United Nations phraseology in a context precisely suited to it. We have seen that inalienability is a characteristic of rights derived not from ordinary international law but from *jus cogens*, customary law so fundamental to the existence of the international community that it can be altered or suspended only with the greatest difficulty. Therefore, by not designating Palestinian rights 'inalienable', the Statement in effect failed to acknowledge that those rights were mandated by *jus cogens*. This left open the possiblity that those rights the Palestinians were entitled to enjoy were not of a fundamental character and were not the product of basic principles but rather of international legal mechanisms operating on a different level. Palestinian rights could, for example, be merely the creation of Security Council resolutions or international treaties and hence subject to limitation or abolition through the same or similar mechanisms. Those rights would then become *ad hoc* and situational rather than essential and absolute. 'Legitimate' rights would then be those which come into being in any given situation through a process of political consensus. Claims on which a consensus could not be reached would never attain legitimacy, never become 'rights'. In practical terms, it would be as if theft were not illegal unless each victim could persuade each thief to acknowledge the illegality.

This may explain how the United States at the time could attempt to allay Israeli fears over the Soviet-American Statement by indicating, in the words of the *New York Times* report, that 'what constitutes Palestinian rights remains to be negotiated'.[37] It may also explain President Carter's statement a few days later to the United Nations General Assembly: 'How these rights are to be *defined ... is, of course, for the interested parties to decide* in detailed negotiations ...'[38] (emphasis supplied).

It is presumably such an analysis of the basis of Palestinian rights which enables the United States to accept, as in the Statement, the existence of the Palestinians as a people and yet reject the possibility of an independent Palestinian state.[39] Foreclosing this possibility has involved Egypt, Israel and the United States in a prolonged and rather awkward dance around the question of Palestinian self-determination.

Thus, when President Carter met with President Sadat at Aswan on January 4, 1978, the two men proposed the so-called 'Aswan formula' which favoured recognition of the legitimate rights of the Palestinian people but only the 'participation' of the Palestinians in the determination of their own future[40] rather than their full responsibility for that determination. Apparently on the basis of this formula American efforts to bring Israel and Egypt to some accord continued throughout the first half of 1978. At one point President Carter was reported in the Israeli press to have put forward the outline of an American plan proposing that at the end of a five-year interim period the inhabitants of the occupied territories would be allowed to vote in a referendum for affiliation with Jordan or Israel, or for a self-rule arrangement similar to that in the Begin Plan, but not for an independent Palestinian state.[41]

Not until September 1978, however, did the Aswan formula seemingly gain Israeli approval in the Camp David Agreements. Paragraph A.1(c) of the Framework for Peace in the Middle East[42] provided that by the end of a five-year transitional period on the West Bank and Gaza the parties were to have reached an agreement recognizing 'the legitimate rights of the Palestinian people and their just requirements', the Palestinians being enabled to 'participate in the determination of their own future' through various mechanisms agreed to in the Framework. However, a close reading of the package of Camp David documents reveals that in fact Israel attempted to avoid acceptance of the Aswan formula. In the Exchange of Letters accompanying the Agreements, President Carter, in a letter dated September 22nd to Prime Minister Begin, was brought to acknowledge that Mr Begin had informed him that the expressions 'Palestinians' or 'Palestinian people' are being and will be construed and understood ... [by Israel] as 'Palestinian Arabs'.[43]

The Israeli reservation embodied in this letter clearly aimed at denying the Palestinians the status of a people, with the possible effect that whatever 'legitimate rights' were to be recognized under the Framework would be those of individuals of a particular ethnic background and not those of an embryonic nation. This Israeli gloss had at least the merit of imposing coherence on the formula's various elements, since, if the Palestinians were to be considered as merely individuals of an ethnic minority, they might more reasonably be told, as the formula seemed to do, that their rights were not absolute but rather a function of their ability to accommodate the state controlling the territory in which they lived. In short, if the Palestinians were not a people, they could more reasonably be limited to mere 'participation', along with Israelis, Egyptians, Jordanians, and Americans, in the determination of their own future.

The contradiction between the Israeli position and that of Egypt persisted in the Egyptian-Israeli Peace Treaty of March 26, 1979,[44] since the parties in the Treaty's preamble merely reaffirmed their adherence to the Camp David Framework for Peace in the Middle East. In the (seemingly inevitable) Exchange of Letters accompanying the Treaty, President Sadat and Prime Minister Begin informed President Carter that they intended to proceed with the implementation of the Framework's provisions relating to the West Bank and the Gaza Strip but they did not indicate any agreement on whose construction or understanding of those provisions would be followed.

The problems of interpretation therefore remained unresolved. So also did the question of the legal effect of the Aswan formula as iterated in the Camp David Framework. Having failed to express its agreement to the American-Egyptian understandings at Aswan and Camp David, Israel may not be bound to them by reason of its own consent. Nevertheless, it is possible on the basis of general legal principles to make the following observations.

Given that self-determination for 'peoples' is a provision of international law to which at the least all United Nations members are bound, and given the Aswan-Camp David formula's recognition of the Palestinians' status as a people, the central element in its legal validity must be the formula's conformity with the norm of self-determination. The modalities of that norm are both doctrinally and logically clear. They are indicated by some of the French equivalents of the English 'self-determination': e.g. *'le droit de libre disposition'* or *'le droit de libre determination'*,[45] that is, *free* disposition or determination by the people affected by the disposition. The point is given legal emphasis in the common first paragraph of the Human Rights Covenants' Article 1:

> All peoples have the right of self-determination. By virtue of the right they freely determine their political status and freely pursue their economic, social and cultural development.[46]

Finally, the International Court of Justice, in its Advisory Opinion in the *Western Sahara Case*, held that

> application of the right of self-determination requires a free and genuine expression of the will of the people concerned.[47]

Indeed, inherent in the concept that people should determine their future for themselves is the requirement that their exercise of that right not be curtailed by extraneous influences. A people either exercises the right or does not, so that some intermediate position, in which self-determination is subject to the determination of others, is vitiated by its own inconsistency. The Aswan-Camp David formula's 'participation' thus does not accord with the requirements of self-determination and is consequently, from the legal perspective, a nullity.

Therefore, Egypt, Israel, and the United States find themselves confronting a full right of Palestinian self-determination, and Israel's refusal to accept that the Palestinians are a people is insignificant in the face of the general international consensus (in which Egypt and the United States join) that they are. The effect is that, regardless of what may have been agreed to at Camp David contrary to the parties' legal obligations, and regardless of attempted Israeli reservations, all parties remain independently bound to implement international law on the matter to ensure that the ultimate disposition of the territories in issue is that desired by the Palestinians themselves. Their central role as a party to the peace process follows logically from this.

But if international law is rigorous on the modalities of self-determination, it is necessarily flexible on the ultimate political choices made in implementation of the principle. Thus the

United Nations General Assembly's declaration on friendly relations and co-operation among states presents a broad spectrum of alternatives:

> The establishment of a sovereign and independent State, the free association or integration with an independent State or the emergence into any other political status freely determined by a people constitute modes of implementing the right of self-determination by that people.[48]

Therefore, although the Palestinians' right to self-determination cannot be the object of *ad hoc* definitions or understandings, the implementation of that right may involve a process of negotiation and consensus depending on the status desired by the Palestinian people itself.

Furthermore, it is conceptually clear that, although the right to self-determination is absolute, the purpose of the right is to raise the embryonic nation to the level of legal equality with other members of the international community but not to give that nation any pre-eminence over them. It is in this spirit that the General Assembly's declaration on friendly relations and co-operation among states, after enunciating the 'principle of equal rights and self-determination', goes on to treat the 'principle of sovereign equality of states' by indicating that all states 'have equal rights *and duties*' (emphasis supplied). In particular,

> (c) Each State has the duty to respect the personality of other States; ...
> (f) Each State has the duty to comply fully and in good faith with its international obligations and to live in peace with other States.[49]

This principle of sovereign equality has long been recognized to be implicit in the United Nations Charter,[50] the same instrument that expressed the principle of self-determination. The two principles should therefore be understood and applied so as to be consistent with each other and with the Charter. As a practical matter this would mean that the evolution of Palestinian self-determination would not be on a one-way street: the Palestinians cannot legally be denied independent statehood if they wish it, but Israel could claim in return that the Palestinian state should shoulder the duties of its new international status.

The focus of peacemaking may then shift to structuring and setting in operation mechanisms to implement the rights of the parties within the framework of international law. On this level the Camp David Agreements made significant advances which deserve careful consideration. But those Agreements do not purport to have resolved all questions, and international law may yet make useful contributions to the ultimate solution. The following chapter examines the Camp David apparatus with a view to determining where it requires modification.

NOTES

1   BROWNLIE, PRINCIPLES OF PUBLIC INTER-NATIONAL LAW 593 (3rd ed.).
2   We are told in Book II of UTOPIA that in the governance of Utopian colonies
    'the natives are allowed to join in if they want to. When this happens, natives and colonists soon combine to form a single community with a single way of life ...'
    MORE, UTOPIA, Paul Turner trans., Penguin Classics edition (1965).
3   54 CONGRESSIONAL RECORD 1742, quoted in THE RIGHT OF SELF-DETERMINATION OF THE PALESTINIAN PEOPLE 2 [U.N. Doc. ST/SG/SER.F/3 (1979)].
4   Cf. BROWNLIE, note 1 *supra*, at 594, referring to the incorporation of the principle of self-determination in the Charter as 'the key development' in its formulation as a legal principle.
5   UNITED NATIONS CHARTER, Article 1, paragraph 5.
6   *Id.*, Article 55.
7   The 'Human Rights Covenants' are:
    The Covenant on Economic, Social and Cultural Rights, Gen. Ass. Res. 2200 (XXI), Dec. 16, 1966, 21 U.N. GAOR Supp. No. 16 (U.N. Doc. A/6316) at 49–52.
    The Covenant on Civil and Political Rights, same as above, at 52–58.
8   BROWNLIE, note 1 *supra*, at 594.
9   *Id.*, at 14.
10 Gen. Ass. Res. 1514 (XV), Dec. 14, 1960, 15 U.N. GAOR, Supp. No. 16 (U.N. Doc. A/4684) at 66.
11 BROWNLIE, note 1 *supra*, at 595.
12 *Id.*, at 594.

13 Advisory Opinion on the Western Sahara Case, [1975] I.C.J. 12, separate opinion of Judge Dillard, at 114.

14 BROWNLIE, note 1 *supra*, at 595.

15 *Id.*, at 513.

16 *Id.*, at 513.

17 *Id.*, at 512.

18 THE RIGHT OF SELF-DETERMINATION OF THE PALESTINIAN PEOPLE, Committee on the Exercise of the Inalienable Rights of the Palestinian People, U.N. Doc. ST/SG/SER.F/3 (1979).

19 *Id.*, at 33–37.

20 Gen. Ass. Res. 3236 (XXIX), November 22, 1974, 29 U.N. GAOR, Supp. 31, at p.4, paragraph 4.

21 Cf. GERSON, ISRAEL, THE WEST BANK AND INTERNATIONAL LAW 206–207.

22 BROWNLIE, note 1 *supra*, at 596.

23 *Id.*, at 75.

24 *Id.*

25 *Id.*, at 68.

26 *See*, for example, M. Merhav, *Peace, or reprieve from decision?*, Jerusalem Post Int'l. Ed., Dec. 27, 1977, at 11.

27 N.Y. Times, June 9, 1979, p.3, cols. 5–6; *see also*, N.Y. Times, May 20, 1979, p.12, cols. 3–6.

28 Int'l. Herald Tribune, Dec. 2–3, 1978, p.2, cols. 7–8.

29 Cf. implicit recognition of this by the International Court of Justice in the Western Sahara Case, note 13 *supra*, in paragraph 59 of the Opinion of the Court.

30 *See*, for example, Y. Blum, *Are the Palestinians 'a people'?*, Jerusalem Post Int'l. Ed., Aug. 16, 1977, at 10.

31 On the history of the early Palestinian national movement, *see* G. ANTONIOUS, THE ARAB AWAKENING 389–412 (Capricorn Books Ed., 1965). *See also*, Chaim Weizmann reported in D. INGRAMS, PALESTINE PAPERS 1917–1922 at 148 as having in 1921 preferred to 'treat the future Palestine as a country where the two nations could live in political harmony and related reciprocally as Palestinian citizens'. Similarly, in 1923, Weizmann is quoted as saying 'In Palestine there is a people which resists our coming', in A. ELON, THE ISRAELIS FATHERS AND SONS 230 (Bantam ed. 1972). *Also* in ELON at 223 an account of Arthur Ruppin who founded the *Brit Shalom*

society to promote a bi-national Palestine.

32 *See* Eban, *Begin's Choice: Peace – or Party Platform*, Washington Post, March 24, 1978, at A21, cols. 1–4.
See, LESCH, POLITICAL ASPIRATIONS OF THE PALESTINIANS ON THE WEST BANK AND THE GAZA STRIP, Chapter 5, section on 'The Sadat Initiative', quoting Weizman: 'we are two peoples (who) are destined to live together in this country ...' in a comment to Israeli radio, June 20, 1978.

33 *See* further on the status of the Palestinians as a people, W.T. & S.V. MALLISON, AN INTERNATIONAL LAW ANALYSIS OF THE MAJOR UNITED NATIONS RESOLUTIONS CONCERNING THE PALESTINE QUESTION 39–41 (U.N. Doc. ST/SG/SER.F/4, United Nations 1979).

34 Text in N.Y. Times, Oct. 2, 1977, p.16, cols. 4–6.

35 N.Y. Times, Oct. 3, 1977, p.6, col. 3.

36 N.Y. Times, Oct. 3, 1977, p.1, col. 6.

37 N.Y. Times, Oct. 4, 1977, p.1.

38 Text in N.Y. Times, Oct. 5, 1977, p. A12, cols. 1–6.

39 *See*, for example, President Carter's answer to a news conference question, transcript in N.Y. Times, May 30, 1979, p.12, cols. 1–6, at col. 6, Question No. 12.

40 Text in N.Y. Times, Jan. 5, 1978, at A4, col. 3.

41 Jerusalem Post Int'l. Ed., March 28, 1978, p.10.

42 Text in 78 DEPT. OF STATE BULL. (Oct., 1978) at 7–9; partial text in N.Y. Times, March 27, 1979, p.A16, cols. 3–6.

43 Letter of Carter to Begin of September 22, 1978, paragraph A. In this same letter, President Carter acknowledged in paragraph B having been informed that 'the expression "West Bank" ... is being, and will be, understood by the Government of Israel as Judea and Samaria'. It is usually assumed that this is merely a distinction in terminology rather than in geographical reference. However, Israeli Minister of Agriculture Sharon has referred in a public statement to Judea, Samaria and the Jordan Valley (Jerusalem Post, Dec. 8, 1978, p.1), thereby seeming to exclude from the West Bank as administered by Jordan before 1967 the section of that area in the Jordan Valley. In this same statement Sharon indicated that Jordan Valley

settlers would not come under Arab administration if the autonomy plan were implemented. The Jordan Valley has in fact been a particular focus of Israeli settlement and 70% of the Valley land north of Jericho is in Israeli hands (LESCH, note 32 *supra*, Chapter 6, section on 'The Impact of Israeli Colonies'), so that significant reasons exist to prompt Israel to exclude the Jordan Valley from the Middle East peace process. In this context, what seem mere terminological discrepancies should not be too lightly dismissed.

44 Dept. of State Publication 8973 (March, 1979).
45 BROWNLIE, note 1 *supra*, at 593 note 4.
46 Gen. Ass. Res. 2200, note 7 *supra*.
47 Western Sahara Case, note 13 *supra*, in paragraph 55.
48 Gen. Ass. Res. 2625 (XXV), Oct. 24, 1970, 25 U.N. GAOR, Supp. No. 28 (U.N. Doc. A/8028) at 121.
49 *Id.*
50 I LAUTERPACHT-OPPENHEIM 413.

6 The Camp David Framework

The Preamble of the Camp David Framework for Peace in the Middle East[1] commits Egypt and Israel to the understanding that the search for peace 'must' be guided by various considerations including: settlement on the basis of Security Council Resolution 242; recognition that the United Nations Charter 'and the other accepted norms of international law and legitimacy' provide 'accepted standards' for international relations; respect for the sovereignty, territorial integrity and political independence 'of every state in the area' within secure and recognized boundaries; recognition that 'security is enhanced by a relationship of peace'; and provision for agreement on the basis of reciprocity to establish 'special security arrangements such as demilitarized zones, limited armaments areas, early warning stations, the presence of international forces, liaison, agreed measures for monitoring, and other arrangements that they agree are useful'.

After recognizing that 'for peace to endure, it must involve all those who have been most deeply affected by the conflict', and stating that the parties 'have agreed to proceed as follows', the Framework goes on in Section A (headed 'West Bank and Gaza') to sketch the apparatus whereby negotiations relating to the West Bank and Gaza should proceed in three stages to achieve the objective that 'Egypt, Israel, Jordan and the representatives of the Palestinian people should participate in negotiations on the resolution of the Palestinian problem in all

115

its aspects.' In view of the intense preoccupation of the Camp
David participants (and particularly Prime Minister Begin[2]) with
verbal distinctions one must assume that this rather convoluted
formulation points to some significant intention of the parties.
For it is not on the face of it apparent why an overall solution of
the 'Palestinian' problem should be reached via three-stage
negotiations on the West Bank and Gaza: one might more
logically expect to see 'resolution of the Palestinian problem in
all its aspects' include the West Bank and Gaza as one aspect.
One might, that is, expect a general solution to lead to particular
applications. That the Camp David formulation seems to
envisage a more inductive process may, however, be consistent
with the parties' reluctance, as previously discussed, to acknowledge absolute Palestinian rights. If this speculation is correct,
the Framework's ordering of the negotiating process is subject to
the criticism already made of the Aswan formula's limitations on
Palestinian self-determination: it possesses in law no binding
force because it inhibits possible Palestinian desires to resolve
the problems of their destiny in some other order.

The legal position with regard to the Framework's detailed
arrangements is more complex. For, to the extent that they are
consistent with Palestinian rights, the arrangements may legally
bind the parties to the Camp David Agreements *inter se* in the
same way that other similar international agreements governed
by the principles of international law are binding.[3] Therefore,
insofar as the Framework established between Israel and Egypt
the legal basis of negotiations on Palestinian autonomy, it set for
the two countries negotiating parameters which in law neither
party can later unilaterally redefine without the consent of the
other party. The question remains, however, how successful the
Framework was in laying such a basis and what that basis is.

Problems of Interpretation

The peculiarities of the Framework's construction lend a certain
challenge to the search for answers. Although, as we have seen,
the Framework purports to delineate a three-stage negotiating
process, with paragraph 1 of Section A divided neatly into
sub-paragraphs (a), (b) and (c) corresponding to those stages, in
fact 'stages' one and two (as formulated in sub-paragraphs (a)

116

and (b)) seem more like two descriptions of the same stage. This perception is discussed further below, but it is useful at this point to consider the consequent implications for the Framework's legal viability.

When problems of interpreting an international agreement arise, the analyst finds a dearth of accepted criteria capable of providing unquestioned standards of interpretation. Article 31 of the Vienna Convention on the Law of Treaties is not yet universally binding and in any case embodies in its 'general rule of interpretation' a standard so 'economical'[4] in its generality that it requires considerable interpretation itself even to begin to be useful. Logic and an appeal to other rules which have in the past been found suitable may provide an acceptable substitute.

Two important interpretive rules have been stated by an authoritative treatise in this way:

> ...It is taken for granted that the contracting parties intend something reasonable and something not inconsistent with generally recognized principles of international law...
> ...It is to be taken for granted that the parties intend the provisions of a treaty to have a certain effect, and not to be meaningless...[5]

It follows that in the case of structural or terminological ambiguity the parties may most reasonably be taken to have intended themselves to be bound by the meaning which is most consistent with international law. Furthermore, the formulation most consistent with international law cannot be vitiated by a seemingly contradictory formulation, since the latter must be read so as not to render the former meaningless. Thus, internal consistency must also be presumed and implemented. Bearing in mind these interpretive principles, one may continue examination of the Framework's text.

Transitional arrangements – first version

Section A.1.(a) provides initially that Egypt and Israel agree to 'transitional arrangements for the West Bank and Gaza for a period not exceeding five years', 'in order to ensure a peaceful and orderly transfer of authority'. The sub-paragraph then states:

> In order to provide full autonomy to the inhabitants, under these arrangements the Israeli military government and its

civilian administration will be withdrawn as soon as a self-governing authority has been freely elected by the inhabitants of these areas to replace the existing military government.

After providing for Jordan to be invited to join negotiations about 'the details of a transitional arrangement', the sub-paragraph ends with the statement that these 'new' arrangements 'should give due consideration' to 'the principle of self-government by the inhabitants' and to the 'legitimate security concerns' of the 'parties' involved.

The plain meaning of the twice-used phrase 'in order to' is to express purpose, and the purposes of the parties are stated in the immediately following clauses: to transfer authority and to provide full autonomy to the inhabitants. The sentence quoted in full above makes unmistakably clear that realization of the second purpose entails free elections followed by withdrawal of the Israeli military government and its civilian administration and their replacement by the freely elected self-governing authority. Given the impermanence international law attaches to belligerent occupation and the recognition accorded the right of self-determination (with which 'full autonomy' is not *prima facie* inconsistent), the two expressed purposes of the parties are compatible with the generally recognized principles of international law, and the stated measures for implementation of the purposes are reasonable in their context. That 'due consideration' should be given to the principle of 'self-government' (again, not *prima facie* inconsistent with self-determination) and to the 'legitimate security concerns' of the 'parties' is therefore also both reasonable, as a secondary concern not conflicting with the sub-paragraph's two purposes, and compatible with international law.

The time sequence of this first stage is worth noting. Under transitional arrangements lasting not more than five years a transfer of authority will take place 'as soon as' the self-governing authority has been freely elected to replace the existing military government which will, with its civilian administration, be withdrawn. Thus one stage would end with the establishment of the self-governing authority and the disappearance of the military government. One would expect that stage two, as presumably set out in sub-paragraph (b), would deal with the transitional period and the negotiations during it over the disposition of the territories at the end of that period.

118

In fact, sub-paragraph (b) states however that Israel, Egypt and Jordan 'will agree' on the modalities for establishing the elected self-governing authority, with Palestinians from the West Bank and Gaza participating as members of the Egyptian or Jordanian delegations to 'negotiate an agreement which will define the powers and responsibilities of the self-governing authority'. The status of the Israeli military government is not mentioned, although 'a withdrawal' of some Israeli forces will take place at some unspecified time, the remaining Israeli forces then being redeployed into 'specified security locations'. 'Arrangements for assuring internal and external security and public order' are to be agreed upon and 'a strong local police force' established. There will be joint Israeli-Jordanian patrols and manning of border control posts.

Echoes of the Begin Plan are numerous in this sub-paragraph, particularly in its military and security references which could be suspected of obliquely including Israeli settlements under the rubric of 'specified security locations'. There could therefore be points in this sub-paragraph that would be capable of bearing constructions putting the provisions in violation of international law. We have seen, however, that the contrary intention by the parties must be presumed and the Framework as a whole, as well as in its particulars, interpreted accordingly. Internal consistency must also be presumed and the document read in that light.

Approaching sub-paragraph (b) in this way, one is first faced with the problem of the three-stage negotiating process: is (b) in fact stage two? There seems no way that agreement 'on the modalities for establishing the elected self-governing authority' could follow the election of that authority nor any way whereby 'an agreement which will define the powers and responsibilities of the self-governing authority' could come after transfer of power to that authority 'as soon as' free elections are held. Sub-paragraph (b) is therefore not stage two, but rather provides details of the developments whose broad outlines are sketched in sub-paragraph (a). The two sub-paragraphs may then be read as consistent. The agreement on powers and responsibilities in (b) must therefore give due consideration to the 'principle of self government' and reflect (a)'s transfer of authority from the withdrawn and replaced military government to the freely elected fully autonomous self-governing authority. Withdrawal of some Israeli forces and redeployment of others cannot run contrary to (a)'s provisions nor can security and police arrangements.[6]

On this basis, certain definite conclusions become possible. The most important is that any arrangements maintaining the Israeli military government in existence would be inconsistent with the Camp David Framework. Egypt and Israel clearly agreed at Camp David that the military government would be replaced and they are bound to each other by that arrangement as it accords with the requirements of international law. It follows further that under the Framework the self-governing authority cannot be so established as to find its constitutional basis in the power of the military government. In proposing both such arrangements the revised Israeli autonomy plan therefore contradicts the letter and spirit of the Camp David Framework.

Israeli Role

Nevertheless, it must be noted that otherwise the Framework in sub-paragraphs (a) and (b) neither endorses nor precludes some legitimate Israeli involvement in the affairs of the territories. However, the absence from the Framework of any favourable references to Israeli claims on sovereignty or legitimacy of settlements, coupled with the invalidity of the former and the illegality of the latter under international law, creates a strong presumption that the Framework did not lay the foundation for any agreement purporting to promote Israeli sovereignty or settlement. Israel therefore could not on the basis of the Framework demand in negotiations on autonomy such presence or involvement. Since Israel agreed to conduct the autonomy negotiations on the basis of the Framework,[7] Israel was precluded from subsequently refusing to carry on negotiations or to bring them to a fruitful conclusion merely because the other parties to the negotiations declined to accept in the occupied territories Israeli sovereignty or settlements. The position therefore appears to have been that, if the Arab negotiators remained firm in rejecting Israeli demands on these two points, Israel had no legal basis to resist conceding both.

Sub-paragraph A.1. (c) moves into what are apparently stages two and three in the Framework's peace process: negotiations 'to determine the final status of the West Bank and Gaza and its relationship with its neighbors' and negotiations 'to conclude a peace treaty between Israel and Jordan by the end of the transitional period' which begins to run upon inauguration of what this sub-paragraph calls 'the self-governing authority (administrative council)'. The status of the West Bank and Gaza is to be the concern of a negotiating committee on which sit 'representatives of the four parties'. Who these 'four parties' are is unclear, since the text speaks only of 'Egypt, Israel, Jordan and the elected representatives of the inhabitants of the West Bank and Gaza'. Representatives evidently do not form a party of their own, nor it is easy to see how the inhabitants as such could individually or collectively be a party in international negotiations. Yet the Framework clearly recognized the existence of a fourth party and it must be identified. Were it not for the Israeli reservation discussed in the preceding chapter, one would be justified in presuming that the Palestinian people was meant. Failing this, the only possible party remaining is the self-governing authority as a legal entity. This reading is consistent with sub-paragraph (a)'s emphasis on full autonomy: the creature of stage one would thereby take on an independent role in the later stages of the negotiating process.

A second, 'related', committee comprising the same parties minus Egypt will negotiate the Israel-Jordanian peace, 'taking into account the agreement reached on the final status of the West Bank and Gaza'.

The two sets of negotiations will be based on 'all the provisions and principles of U.N. Security Council Resolution 242' and will 'resolve, among other matters, the location of the boundaries and the nature of the security arrangements'.

Equitable Implications

Finally, as was discussed above, the 'solution from the negotiations must also recognize the legitimate rights of the Palestinian people and their just requirements'. The phrase 'legitimate rights' and the legal objections to it have been examined, but it is appropriate to consider at this point what is the import of the added phrase 'just requirements'. As a matter of interpretation one must assume that the latter phrase is not mere excess verbiage but in fact is meant to add to the bundle of benefits accorded the Palestinians something that 'legitimate rights' (understood as involving legal entitlements) do not confer. The use of the word 'just' suggests that the parties to the Framework had in mind the ancient distinction between legal rights and justice, between law and equity. The distinction has retained in the law of nations the principled character it has unfortunately lost in Anglo-Saxon domestic jurisprudence, so that settled rules of international law may be moderated through equity by 'considerations of fairness, reasonableness, and policy'[8] or by taking account of special circumstances in a case.[9] It has been observed that this exceptional character implies that decisions made on the basis of equity 'admit of no generalization and cannot contribute to the formation of rules of international law'.[10]

Precisely what may be considered to come under the rubric of 'just requirements' is difficult to determine since the Palestinians have generally couched their demands in terms of inalienable legal rights not subject to limitation by the sort of *ad hoc* considerations of policy which equity may recognize. From this perspective 'just requirements' may be viewed as reinforcing that restriction of Palestinian entitlements which we have already seen to be implicit in the concept of 'legitimate rights'. On the other hand, the introduction of equity into the disposition of the Palestinian problem may represent an attempt by the parties to the Framework to permit *ad hoc* resolution of particular issues ostensibly without establishing juridical precedents which would bind them in resolving legally similar, but politically more difficult, questions. The problem of Jerusalem comes to mind in this context. Although it is unlikely that Palestinians could find the 'just requirements' formula theoretically acceptable in either of its applications, one must acknowledge its possible utility in allowing practical improvements in the Palestinian condition.

A similarly qualified judgement may be reached on the Framework's provisions for displaced persons and refugees.

In the background of these provisions was Article 21 of the original Begin Plan which envisaged the establishment of a Jordanian-Israeli Administrative Council committee to determine for the West Bank and Gaza by unanimous agreement 'norms of immigration' and 'the norms whereby Arab refugees residing outside' those areas 'will be permitted to immigrate...in reasonable numbers'. The language used, when read in conjunction with the blanket authorization in Article 20 of the Begin Plan for settlement by Israelis, signifies that all non-Israelis, even those who are Palestinians by birth and former residence, if they are not already living in the areas, are to be treated as if they were nothing more than potential 'immigrants', i.e., aliens possessing no legal right of entry or residence who are permitted to reside in the areas as a matter of grace – or of politics – and who may be subject to deportation at the discretion of the government.[11]

Palestinians who are specifically 'refugees' (whether from 1948 or 1967) fare no better and are indeed subject to a quota based on what the committee decides are 'reasonable numbers' of immigrants. Article 21 clearly did not implement any 'inalienable rights'.

Displaced persons and refugees distinguished

The Framework in contrast eschews the term 'immigration' and hence avoids many of that term's legal implications as to the discretionary power of the relevant authority to refuse Palestinians entry or to expel them as aliens. Furthermore, paragraphs A.3 and A.4 distinguish between the problem of those persons who were displaced as a result of the 1967 war from the West Bank and Gaza and 'the refugee problem' (presumably encompassing those persons displaced from areas under Israeli control since 1948). The practical rationale for such a distinction is clear: the return home of persons displaced from the West Bank and Gaza in no way entails the sort of disruptive reintegration of Palestinians directly into the Jewish State which Israel has claimed to fear from a return of the 1948 refugees to their homes.[12] A legal basis for the distinction derives from the fact that, while the right of return of the 1948 refugees is maintained in a series of United Nations General Assembly resolutions beginning with Resolution 194 of December 11, 1948 (discussed further below), the right of the 1967 displaced persons to go back to their homes is supported by a call for Israeli compliance in Security Council Resolution 237 of June 14, 1967.[13] The legal significance of this varying treatment by United Nations organs may be clarified by a brief consideration of the role of the Security Council under the United Nations Charter.

Chapter VII of the Charter governs the mandatory actions which the security council may take when confronted with breaches of, or threats to, international peace and security. In such circumstances the Council is empowered by Articles 39 and 41 to decide on measures to restore or maintain that peace and security and 'to call upon the Members of the United Nations to apply such measures' (Article 41). Furthermore, in conjunction with the powers of Articles 39 and 41, Article 40 provides:

> In order to prevent an aggravation of the situation, the Security Council may, before making the recommendations or deciding upon the measures provided for in Article 39, call upon the parties concerned to comply with such provisional measures as it deems necessary or desirable.

Since Article 25 of the Charter embodies the agreement of all United Nations members 'to accept and carry out the decisions of the Security Council', decisions (as opposed to mere recommendations) by the Council under Chapter VII are binding on all members. However even mere recommendations may 'provide requisite authority for individual or collective action in pursuance of the Charter'.[14]

Resolution 237's preambulatory statement of the considerations which motivated the Council's decision to adopt the resolution brings the document within Chapter VII. One consideration was the existence of 'an urgent need to spare the civil population... additional suffering' – an expression which, in its implication of necessity and its reference to 'additional suffering' (which could aggravate a still-evolving situation and hence jeopardize further Council measures), may reasonably be read as invoking Article 40. Another consideration was that 'essential and inalienable human rights should be respected even during the vicissitudes of war'. This language indicates that the

124

Council intended through its resolution to deal with a situation in which war was still inflicting its suffering on individuals, in which the June war's breach of the peace had not yet been definitively halted. This intention accorded well with the situation on the ground as of June 14, 1967. A tenuous general cease-fire had only been effectively imposed on the parties three days earlier (through Council Resolution 236 of June 11) and within a few weeks was to break down in renewed warfare on the Suez Canal front. In the occupied territories obliteration of some villages and large parts of certain towns and expulsion of the inhabitants were being carried out by Israeli military forces after the cessation of fighting. In a real sense Israel was continuing to wage war on the civilian population even after general hostilities had ended. Furthermore, the contemporaneous Palestinian exodus from the occupied territories (often encouraged by Israel), when coupled with the misery of those who had fled during the fighting and could not return, was augmenting the potential for further disruptions of the peace.[15]

In this light the effect of Resolution 237 is clear. In paragraph 1 the Council

> *Calls upon* the Government of Israel to facilitate the return of those inhabitants who have fled the areas [where military operations have taken place] since the outbreak of hostilities. [emphasis in original]

This language is not that of recommendation. Where the Council intended merely to recommend, as in paragraph 2, it said so explicitly with specific words to that effect. It is reasonable to infer in that context that, when the Council in paragraph 1 used the 'call upon' language of Articles 40 and 41, it aimed to impose an obligation consonant with its Chapter VII powers and responsibilities for the restoration of international peace and security.

A further legal justification for the Council's obligatory call upon Israel may be found in those 'essential and inalienable human rights' to which the resolution's preamble referred. For the Universal Declaration of Human Rights,[16] regarded often as part of the law of the United Nations[17] and considered a guide to the content of 'fundamental rights and freedoms as understood by members of the United Nations',[18] provides in Article 13:

> Everyone has the right to leave any country, including his own, and to return to his country.

This right has been given further international recognition in the second of the Human Rights covenants, that on Civil and Political Rights,[19] which states in Article 12(4):

No one shall be arbitrarily deprived of the right to enter his own country.

In the case of persons whose departure from the occupied territories was caused by Israeli actions in violation of Article 49 of the Fourth Geneva Convention, the right of return is a necessary corollary to this other generally accepted rule of international law. In any case, the right well reflects the spirit of the Fourth Geneva Convention's provisions, including Article 49, and it accords with the decades-long movement of international law towards amelioration of the condition of stateless persons and refugees.[20]

Therefore, when the Framework distinguished between those driven out in 1948 and those who fled in 1967, it usefully highlighted once again an important Palestinian legal advantage which the Begin Plan had obscured. Israel's acceptance of the Framework's distinction represents a legally binding commitment to it and a contradiction of the Begin Plan's categorizations on immigration. The Framework thus laid the basis for negotiations between Israel and the Arabs not on the question of whether the 1967 displaced persons have a right to return – as we have seen, an affirmative answer derives from the very basis of the Framework's distinction – but merely on the means and procedures for giving effect to that right.[21] Paragraph A.3 of the Framework seems to say as much:

During the transitional period, representatives of Egypt, Israel, Jordan, and the self-governing authority will constitute a continuing committee to decide by agreement on the modalities of admission to persons displaced from the West Bank and Gaza in 1967, together with necessary measures to prevent disruption and disorder.

That this committee's mandate reaches only to the 'modalities of admission' confines its work to decisions on the practical implementation of an already agreed policy to admit. The Framework gives the committee no power to remake policy or to impose quotas or other general limitations on displaced Palestinians wishing to return home. The only potentially restrictive power conferred by the Framework is that to decide, 'together with' its decisions on the modalities of admission, on 'measures to prevent disruption and disorder'. In terms of paragraph A.3, the need for such public safety measures can arise only as a consequence of the admission of displaced persons. It follows that the power to decide on such measures does not possess independent status but is dependent on, and subordinate to, the power to decide on modalities of admission. That decisions on measures should be taken only 'together with', not independently of, decisions on modalities emphasizes this subordination. More concretely, the typical question before the committee would not be 'Should we decline to admit in order to avoid disruption and disorder?' but rather 'Faced with the inevitablity of admission, how can we see it accomplished without disruption and disorder?' In short, the committee's public safety power would provide no pretext for obstructing admission.

'Refugees'

But although the Framework offers a viable plan for the return home of the 1967 displaced persons, the same cannot be said of the provision on the refugees of 1948. The language of paragraph A.4 deserves quotation in full:

> Egypt and Israel will work with each other and with other interested parties to establish agreed procedures for a prompt, just and permanent implementation of the resolution of the refugee problem.

This sentence echoes paragraph 2(b) of Security Council Resolution 242[22] which affirms the necessity for 'achieving a just settlement of the refugee problem'. But the Framework at first appears to reflect such progress towards settlement that issues of principle are no longer in dispute and the parties now need only work to establish agreed 'procedures' for implementation much as they had merely to agree on 'modalities of admission' in paragraph A.3. Equity reappears in the requirement that implementation be 'just', suggesting perhaps a balancing of competing interests – a process not necessarily inconsistent with the choice of return or compensation provided for Palestinian refugees under paragraph 11 of General Assembly Resolution 194.[23] Furthermore, by providing a more flexible negotiating structure than the quadripartite committee of paragraph A.3, the Framework seems to recognize that there may be 'other interested parties', beyond the committee's four, willing, able and entitled to be involved in, and contribute to, implementation. Thus far paragraph A.4 embodies positive progress in dealing with the refugee issue.

But what is one to make of the provision's last seven words? The greenest first-year law student is exhorted to eschew ambiguity[24] and to become the master of 'proper words in proper places'.[25] Calculated ambiguity is accepted only with troubled conscience as the price of reconciling reasonable and unreasonable men.[26] To speculate in this vein on the motives of the Camp David participants would be invidious, but one cannot avoid the realization that paragraph A.4's conclusion attains a level of confusion that perhaps owes more to diplomacy than to legal draftsmanship. For while the sentence makes reasonable sense up to the word 'implementation' it then collapses into a semantic tangle. As one reads on, one expects an answer to the question: 'Implementation of what?' At first the response seems to be: 'of *the* resolution *on* the refugee problem', i.e., General Assembly Resolution 194 permitting the return or compensation choice. But the words used are in fact 'the resolution *of* the refugee problem'. The Framework therefore does not use 'resolution' in the sense of 'decision' but perhaps with the meaning 'solution'. Now, if 'solution' here means 'the act or process of solving', 'implementation' would seem to become redundant: one need not agree on procedures to implement the act of solving but simply on procedures for that act.[27] Indeed, one can simply agree on the act itself which would appear necessarily to imply its own procedures. And yet, if 'solution' does not have this meaning, the alternative significance is 'answer', to which the analyst may well respond 'What answer?' There is certainly no provision in paragraph A.4 for agreement on a resolution in that sense and yet, as noted above, the prior existence of such an agreement is implicit in the paragraph's concentration on procedure. But where, then, is that 'resolution'?

The Jordanian Role

One searches the Framework in vain for an explicit statement of that 'answer'. However, a glimmer of indirect light may be

128

discerned in paragraph A.1(c) which provides *inter alia* that a peace treaty is to be concluded between Israel and Jordan through negotiations 'based on *all* the provisions and principles of U.N. Security Council Resolution 242' (emphasis supplied). As noted above, one of those provisions is a call for 'a just settlement of the refugee problem'. If this is indeed where the 'resolution' must be sought, the implications are serious. For if the resolution of the refugee problem is to be a function of the relations between Jordan and Israel, Jordan and the Palestinians (not to mention the 'other interested parties' to whom paragraph A.4 refers) could find themselves forced to accept the oft-repeated Israeli claim that 'Geographically and ethnically Jordan is Palestine'.[28]

Historical Antecedents to the Israeli Claim

As a matter of fact this claim evinces a perverse disregard for the realities of the area. The geographical argument is plainly ridiculous[29] and the anthropological argument is almost on a par with the geographical. Raphael Patai more than two decades ago stated[30] the facts on this point with clarity:

> One of the basic cultural features of the Kingdom of Jordan is the difference between the old residents of the East Bank... and the people of the West Bank...
> ...With regard to descent and historical antecedents...there are definite differences between the population of the two Banks...[31]
> ... with regard to ecology and cultural background considerable differences exist between the population of the West Bank and of the East Bank...[32]
> ...[The Jordanian annexation of the West Bank] brought together two population elements greatly differing from each other in numerous respects...[33]
> ...the Palestinian Arab population as a whole...constituted a group much more advanced in Westernization than their fellow-citizens to the east of the river...[34]
> ...The annexation added urban centers with their educated and semi-educated citizenry to rural and largely illiterate Transjordan...[35]

An historical Palestinian identity separate from that of the Jordanians is explicit in Patai's statement that the 'Jordanians of today are the sons and grandsons of people who, *together with* the Syrians, *Arab Palestinians*, and Iraqis, formed the Arab population of the Ottoman Empire'[36] (emphasis supplied). This observation highlights another important point: before the infusion of Palestinians into Jordan in 1948 there resided on the East Bank some 400,000 non-Palestinian Jordanians.[37] That these latter and the Palestinians by and large share a common language and religion no more obliges them to accept political union than a similar inheritance requires the Walloons of Belgium to form a union with France or Anglophone Canadians to join the United States. Indeed, even if the Palestinians and Jordanians were identical in every respect, the only justification in law for their submission to a common political regime would be that they themselves freely so choose. This is the essence of the principle of self-determination.

What, then, is the significance of the continued Israeli insistence that 'Jordan is Palestine'? The historical background of the answer to this question has been examined and documented by Erskine Childers in his contribution to the study *The Transformation of Palestine.*[38] He notes the recollection of Sir Alec Kirkbride, a British official in Palestine and Transjordan during the 1920s and later, that at least initially the pro-Zionist British Mandate administration intended parts of the East Bank in Transjordan

> to serve as a reserve of land for use in the resettlement of Arabs once the National Home for Jews in Palestine...became an accomplished fact.[39]

Childers goes on to demonstrate that this thinking was reflected in Zionist policy on what Chaim Weizmann in 1937 called 'transfer of the Arab population' of Palestine.[40] In 1942 Weizmann indicated that the 'transfer' could be voluntary.[41] But the outbreak of Zionist terrorism – which, when it was directed against British interests, Winston Churchill characterized as 'a new wave of banditry worthy of the Nazi Germans'[42] – changed the course of Palestinian history.

Childers shows that terrorizing of the Arab population of Palestine in 1948 was widespread and well-organized and not confined to the terrorist organizations of Menachem Begin and others but was also practised by the official Zionist military organization, the Haganah.[43] Evidence is provided for the conclusion that by the end of the Mandate on May 15, 1948, if not before, the removal of Arab civilians had become an Israeli war aim.[44]

A principal instance of the Israeli 'transfer' of the Arab population was that of the two Arab towns of Ramleh and Lydda. Childers records that Israeli loudspeaker vans toured the captured towns announcing that the Arab inhabitants had forty-eight hours to get out of Transjordan.[45] That 50,000 Palestinians had been expelled from Ramleh and Lydda was for many years vigorously denied by Israeli apologists. What must surely be the definitive refutation of those denials has come recently from the commander of the Israeli army unit responsible, former Prime Minister Yitzhak Rabin. In a passage of his memoirs which was censored in Israel but later published *in extenso* in the *New York Times*,[46] Rabin wrote of a meeting between himself, Yigael Allon, and the then Prime Minister David Ben-Gurion, and he described the consequences of that meeting:

> While the fighting was still in progress, we had to grapple with a troublesome problem for whose solution we could not draw upon any previous experience: the fate of the civilian population of Lod and Ramle, numbering some 50,000.
>
> We walked outside, Ben-Gurion accompanying us. Allon repeated his question: 'What is to be done with the population?' B.G. waved his hand in a gesture which said 'Drive them out!'
>
> Allon and I held a consultation. I agreed that it was essential to drive the inhabitants out. We took them on foot towards the Bet Horon Road, assuming that the [Jordanian] legion would be obliged to look after them...
>
> 'Driving out' is a term with a harsh ring. Psychologically this was one of the most difficult actions we undertook. The population of Lod did not leave willingly. There was no way of avoiding the use of force and warning shots in order to make the inhabitants march the 10 to 15 miles to the point where they met up with the legion.
>
> The inhabitants of Ramle watched and learned the lesson. Their leaders agreed to be evacuated voluntarily, on condition that the evacuation was carried out by vehicles. Buses took them to Latrun, and from there, they were evacuated by the legion.
>
> Great suffering was inflicted on the men taking part in the eviction action. Soldiers of the Yiftach Brigade included youth-movement graduates, who had been inculcated with values such as international brotherhood and humaneness. The eviction action went beyond the concepts they were used to.
>
> There were some fellows who refused to take part in the

expulsion action. Prolonged propaganda activities were required after the action, to remove the bitterness of these youth movement groups, and explain why we were obliged to undertake such a harsh and cruel action.

When the 1948 'transfer' was completed, some 780,000 Palestinians found themselves refugees.[47] Following the 1967 Middle East war, approximately 400,000 people fled from Gaza and the West Bank to East Jordan.[48] Although he would dispute the magnitude of these figures, Yaacov Shimoni, a student of the question and an official in the Israeli Foreign Ministry, has offered statistics which indicate clearly that only a minority of 44% of the total refugees from both wars remained within the boundaries of mandate Palestine while 56% went elsewhere.[49] By Shimoni's figures it would only be possible to say that a majority of the refugees had remained 'in Palestine' if one considered the East Bank of Jordan within that rubric, in which case 83% of Shimoni's total would have remained in Palestine.[50]

These Israeli figures are an important indicator of the significance of the 'Jordan is Palestine' argument. They provide the evident foundation and explanation for the otherwise inexplicable statement of Israeli United Nations Ambassador Yosef Tekoah to the General Assembly in 1974 that

the vast majority of Palestinian refugees never left Palestine, but moved, as a result of the 1948 and 1967 wars, from one part of the country to another.[51]

On the basis of Shimoni's statistics Tekoah's statement could only be correct if East Jordan were part of Palestine. Even aside from the statistics, it is obvious that none of the 1967 refugees fled either into Israel or to the West Bank or Gaza but rather fled from those areas into East Jordan and could not therefore be said to have fled 'from one part of the country to another' unless Palestine included East Jordan.

The implications of such an internal 'transfer' are of the utmost significance, as Tekoah emphasized:

It is therefore false to allege that the Palestinian people has been deprived of a State of its own or that it has been uprooted from its national homeland...[52]

The purpose and consequences of identifying the East Bank as part of Palestine begin to become clear: they include denying the very legal existence of the refugee problem and absolving Israel of guilt for the 'politicide' of Arab Palestine. A Palestinian state is still in existence, so the argument runs, and, since refugees are usually understood to be persons who have for various reasons sought safety outside the country of their nationality,[53] Palestinians who are still in their own country are *ipso facto* not uprooted refugees at all. Implicit in Tekoah's argument is the further consequence that Palestinians who are in their own country would have no right of return to their former homes and their claims to compensation for loss of their real property would appear much weakened also.

Furthermore, if Jordan is Palestine, indeed can only be Palestine (since, by the Israeli argument, Jordan would have had no claim at all to statehood until it was included with the originally-proposed area of the Palestine Mandate), then its citizens must be 'Palestinians'. But what if the Jordanians or Palestinians reject this identity? Tekoah's answer is blunt: 'without the Palestinians, Jordan is a state without a people'.[54] The significance of this is not that Jordan would otherwise be a country without a population, but rather that the inhabitants who are there would not constitute a 'people' in the legal sense discussed above. The inhabitants would then arguably have no rights as a people to assert against an existing people that did claim rights in the territory. The advantage which would then accrue to Israel is not hard to discover.

For Tekoah's language sounds with disconcerting resonance the same note as struck by early Zionists when they sought to justify their claims on the Holy Land by describing Palestine as a land without a people for a people without a land.[55] In that context, one is reminded that the Zionist Organization proposed to the Paris Peace Conference of 1919 that the boundaries of the Jewish National Home should extend to the Litani River in the north, almost to Damascus in the north-east, and to the Hejaz Railway in the east (i.e., encompassing most of the fertile land of East Jordan).[56] Even after Transjordan was definitively severed from the Palestine Mandate in 1922, Zionist interest in it remained, so that David Ben-Gurion could tell the Seventeenth Zionist Congress in 1931:

In eastern Palestine, there are broader and emptier acres...we are entitled to ask the right to enter Transjordan...[57]

This concept of Jordan as 'eastern Palestine' remains alive in the philosophy of Prime Minister Begin's Herut Party, the dominant element in the Likud government of Israel. The Likud platform in the 1977 election which brought Begin to power declared:

> The right of the Jewish people to Eretz-Israel [i.e., 'the land of Israel', not synonymous with the State of Israel] is eternal, unshakable, and is combined with the right to security and peace...[58]

The platform went on to indicate that in peace negotiations the Likud would not concede any 'parts of *western* Eretz-Israel' (emphasis supplied) whose boundary was the Jordan river – thereby clearly implying that beyond the Jordan lay 'eastern Eretz-Israel', presumably a portion of that whole Eretz-Israel to which the Jewish people has an 'eternal, unshakable' right. As recently as May 1979 Prime Minister Begin reiterated the concept of 'western' Eretz-Israel.[59]

Of course, one should not attach undue importance to utterances inspired by party ideology. But when one sees Israeli protégés on the banks of the Litani, and Israeli troops still only a few miles south-west of Damascus (and apparently intending to remain there indefinitely) one is entitled not to dismiss as totally irrelevant implicit Israeli interest in 'eastern Palestine'. And there is certainly no reason at all for Jordan or the Palestinians to encourage such sentiments or give any legal recognition to them.

Thus the 'Jordan is Palestine' argument can be seen as an attempt to lay the basis for eliminating the legal claims of the Palestinians as a people and as individual refugees while at the same time providing in the alternative for an Israeli claim against Jordan.

Thus there are a number of fundamental issues associated with the idea of settling the refugee problem by turning Jordan into Palestine, and there are good reasons for both Jordan and the Palestinians to wish to avoid negotiating on such an idea.

In allowing vagueness and ambiguity on the refugee question to leave open possibilities so likely to discourage Jordanian and Palestinian participation, and in failing to promote Palestinian interest by reiterating the return-or-compensation alternative on which the international community has been generally agreed in the past,[60] the Framework evidences its greatest failure. At best the Framework on this point makes a solution acceptable to the Palestinians highly improbable.

Conclusion

In summary, then, the Framework, though establishing principles and mechanisms whereby a settlement might be reached, was marred by serious and potentially vitiating faults. An imaginative and comprehensive peace plan fully implementing the requirements of international law remained to be adumbrated.

NOTES

1   78 DEPT. OF STATE BULLETIN (Oct. 1978) at pp.7–9 and N.Y. Times, March 27, 1979, p.A16, cols. 3–6 for texts of Camp David Agreements.
2   Cf. for example, report in N.Y. Times, March 12, 1978, Sect. 4 at 2, cols. 3–5.
3   *See*, in general, BROWNLIE, PRINCIPLES OF PUBLIC INTERNATIONAL LAW (3rd ed.) 600–632, and in particular on *pactum de contrahendo* I LAUTERPACHT-OPPENHEIM 890–891.
4   BROWNLIE, note 3 *supra*, at 625.
5   I LAUTERPACHT-OPPENHEIM 952, 955.
6   The same reading must also be given to the following Section A.2 which assures that 'all necessary measures' be taken for Israel's security during the transition period 'and beyond'. This would be done in part by the self-governing authority's establishing a strong local police force which will maintain 'continuing liaison on internal security matters' with Egyptian, Israeli and Jordanian officers. A considerable degree of autonomy in internal security matters must therefore be presumed.
7   *See* letter of Sadat and Begin to Carter dated March 26, 1979 and included in the Peace Treaty exchange of letters.
8   BROWNLIE, note 3 *supra*, at 27.
9   SØRENSEN, ed., MANUAL OF PUBLIC INTERNATIONAL LAW 152, in Chapter on 'The Sources of International Law' by M. Virally.
10 *Id.*, and cf., BROWNLIE, note 3 *supra*, at 27.

11   I LAUTERPACHT-OPPENHEIM 675–676, 691–695.

12   *See*, for example, the letter of August 1, 1948 from Israeli Foreign Minister Shertok to the United Nations Mediator, Count Bernadotte, in Progress Report of the UN Mediator in Palestine, 3 GAOR Supp. (No. 11) 27–28, U.N. Doc. A/648 (1948), reprinted in THE RIGHT OF RETURN OF THE PALESTINIAN PEOPLE, U.N. Doc. ST/SG/SER. F/2, at pages 48–50 (Nov. 1978).

13   S.C. Res. 237, 22 U.N. SCOR Resolutions (U.N. Doc. S/INF/22/Rev.2) at 5.

14   I LAUTERPACHT-OPPENHEIM 429.

15   Cf. WILSON, JERUSALEM KEY TO PEACE 111–114; SCHLEIFER, THE FALL OF JERUSALEM, 205–212, 218–219, 221–222, 228. The present writer's first-hand observation on the West Bank during and after the June war generally accords with the information given by the two authors cited, particularly with regard to the devastation in Beit Awa (which the present writer was the first outsider to discover) and in Yalu, Beit Nuba, and Imwas.

16   General Assembly Resolution 217 of December 10, 1948, 3 GAOR Resolutions, U.N. Doc. A/810 p.71.

17   BROWNLIE, note 3 *supra*, at 571.

18   BRIERLY, THE LAW OF NATIONS 294 (6th ed.) Cf. also, SØRENSEN, note 9 *supra*, at 501, in chapter on 'The Individual in International Law' by S. Oda.

19   Adopted by General Assembly Resolution 2200 of December 16, 1966, 21 GAOR Supp. 16 (A/6316) pp.52–58.

20   Cf. I LAUTERPACHT-OPPENHEIM 669–675.

21   Cf. statement by Assistant Secretary of State Saunders in 78 DEPT. OF STATE BULLETIN (November 1978) at p.44, col.1, tending to confirm the distincton and the interpretation suggested here.

22   S.C. Res. 242, 22 U.N. SCOR Resolutions, U.N. Doc. S/INF/22/Rev.2 at 8–9 (November 22, 1967).

23   Gen. Ass. Resolution 194, 3 U.N. GAOR Resolutions (U.N. Doc. A/810) pp.21–25 (December 11, 1948).

24   WEIHOFEN, LEGAL WRITING STYLE 84, 255–257.

25   BIRKETT, SIX GREAT ADVOCATES 108.

26   MELLINKOFF, THE LANGUAGE OF THE LAW 450.

27   Significantly, in testimony before a Congressional committee, Assistant Secretary of State Saunders paraphrased

this sentence so as to remove the redundancy, note 21 *supra*.

28 Y. TEKOAH, IN THE FACE OF THE NATIONS 155.

29 *See* HOADE, GUIDE TO THE HOLY LAND 1 (8th ed.), Franciscan Printing Press, Jerusalem (1976): Jordan is separated from Palestine by the Jordan Rift Valley, a 'huge depression...which for its depth is unique...[and which] divides the country into two well defined parts, Palestine and Transjordan'.

30 PATAI, THE KINGDOM OF JORDAN.

31 *Id.*, at 13.

32 *Id.*, at 16.

33 *Id.*, at 50.

34 *Id.*, at 51.

35 *Id.*, at 238.

36 *Id.*, at 280.

37 *Id.*, at 10.

38 THE TRANSFORMATION OF PALESTINE 165 and ff., I. Abu Lughod, ed., (1971).

39 *Id.*, at 173.

40 *Id.*, at 176.

41 *Id.*, at 176.

42 Quoted in BELL, TERROR OUT OF ZION 158 (Avon Discus paperback ed., 1978).

43 TRANSFORMATION, note 38 *supra*, at 183–196.

44 *Id.*, at 185 and 194.

45 *Id.*, at 195.

46 N.Y. Times, Oct. 23, 1979, p.A3, cols. 1–6.

47 *See* Janet Abu Lughod, 'The Demographic Transformation of Palestine', in THE TRANSFORMATION OF PALESTINE 139, at 161 (note 38 *supra*).

48 *Id.*, at 163.

49 *See* POLITICAL DICTIONARY OF THE MIDDLE EAST IN THE 20th CENTURY, revised ed., eds. Shimoni, Levine, Rabinovich and Shaked (1974) *sub voc* 'Refugees', in which Shimoni suggests the following distribution of Palestinian refugees:

	1948 War	1967 War	Totals
To			
West Bank	200,000	—	200,000
Gaza Strip	200,000	—	200,000
Transjordan	100,000	250,000	350,000
Syria, Lebanon &			
elsewhere	150,000	—	150,000
	650,000	250,000	900,000

By these figures, 400,000 refugees would have remained within the 1948 borders of Palestine while 500,000 would have gone beyond those borders.

50   If the figures shown in note 49 for Transjordan are added to those for the West Bank and the Gaza Strip the total for these areas would then be 750,000 refugees out of a total 900,000.

51   TEKOAH, note 28 *supra*, at 155.

52   *Id.*, at 156.

53   Cf. I LAUTERPACHT-OPPENHEIM 672.

54   TEKOAH, note 28 *supra*, at 155.

55   D. PERETZ, THE MIDDLE EAST TODAY 251 (2nd ed.). *See* also Childers in THE TRANSFORMATION OF PALESTINE, note 38 *supra*, at 168.

56   D. INGRAMS, PALESTINE PAPERS 1917–1922, at 52.

57   Quoted in THE TRANSFORMATION OF PALESTINE, note 38 *supra*, at 21.

58   Quoted in Amit, 'Israeli Politics and Peace in the Middle East', WAR OR PEACE IN THE MIDDLE EAST 96, at 108, P. Duff ed. (1978).

59   N.Y. Times, May 3, 1979, p.A5, col.1.

60   Cf. the comment on this point by Mayor Milhem of Halhul in NEWSWEEK, July 9, 1979, p.15.

7   Thoughts on a Settlement: Lessons from the Austrian Example

It was the hope of American policy-makers that the Camp David Framework would 'set in motion a political and psychological dynamic capable of transforming this terrible conflict'.[1] If Camp David succeeded in stimulating that dynamic, it did not, as we have seen, establish a clear goal in relation to the Palestinian question such that the dynamic could lead to a legally viable peace with which the Palestinians could live. Several observers have suggested that the goal may be attained by a solution modelled on the arrangements whereby Austria was enabled to resume her independent status in 1955.[2]

Historical comparisons are often dangerous because unique circumstances in each case are frequently incomparable or hard to assess. But the international lawyer may not for that reason shirk the duty to sift out the irrelevant and determine whether, and to what extent, past experience may have established legally significant precedent. Approached in this spirit, the Austrian experience has much to tell.

Parallels between the Austrian and West Bank-Gaza situations abound: previous international status as part of recognized entities, rule by a country later defeated in war, occupation by the victors, and finally negotiation of peace with those victors for some status differing from any previously experienced.[3] But far more important similarities are those which could link the re-establishment of Austrian independence and the achievement of

Palestinian self-determination. Austrian statehood was restored partly because all the parties in the negotiations needed to conclude a peace treaty, each was willing to assure the others as to their security interests and legal rights in the context of a comprehensive settlement, the Austrians were willing to accept limitations on the country's freedom of action on the international level in exchange for the psychological and political advantages to be gained, and the international community was able to apply its legal doctrine flexibly to permit an acceptable treaty to be drawn up and implemented.[4]

Indispensable also was the role of the Austrians themselves. The four occupying powers had in 1946 recognized a very broad measure of Austrian self-government[5] which legitimized immediate post-war developments whereby 'a surprising number of Austrians' had been able 'to come forward and run the country's affairs'.[6] In consequence, when the negotiations on the Austrian State Treaty reached their critical stage nine years later, there were recognized representative institutions which could speak in the name of Austria to reassure the other parties to the negotiations about Austria's future intentions in Europe.[7] It is important to note on this point that the recognition of these institutions was not given by any of the victorious Allies except after determined efforts by the Austrians first to resolve their own internal political differences (which had before 1938 been bitter and divisive)[8] and then to bring to bear their own toughness and political ingenuity[9] to exploit to their advantage whatever opportunities arose. Thus, the 'part played by the Austrians themselves... was important and probably decisive'.[10] After a decade of effort the result was the re-establishment in 1955 of a sovereign, independent and democratic Austrian state[11] committed to perpetual neutrality[12] and to restrictions on the composition and equipment of her armed forces.[13]

The Preamble of the Camp David Framework recognized that 'representatives of the Palestinian people should participate in negotiations on the resolution of the Palestinian problem'. But, as we have seen, participation does not equal self-determination and a selection from choices dictated by others is not democracy. Furthermore, even if the arrangements for the occupied territories were completely unobjectionable, they would still give no voice to the majority of Palestinians who live outside those territories.[14] This leaves most Palestinians without a voice, but even more seriously it does not recognize a representative of the Palestinians who can commit them all to a binding agreement. There is at present therefore no institution which can claim to occupy a place like that of the Austrian government in the decade before 1955.

The Framework, of course, provides for the establishment of a self-governing authority. To the extent that it would enjoy genuinely 'full autonomy' it could fill the role of a local representative institution for those Palestinians living on the West Bank and Gaza. Unfortunately, the authority's essentially local and limited character would, even in the best of circumstances, preclude its functioning as the representative of the Palestinian people as a whole. Furthermore, insofar as it might be generally hampered or circumscribed by the restrictive provisions of the Israeli autonomy Plan, the authority would be in every sense incompetent to bind even those Palestinians under its administration. The parties to the negotiations on the future of Palestine could thus find themselves negotiating in a vacuum in which no significant indigenous representative speaks for Palestine.

This poses a serious problem for all the parties to the Camp David Agreements but for none more than for Israel. For if Israel insists on restrictions which would make the self-governing authority a dead letter before it began, it will become apparent that no alternative exists but to turn to that representative which Palestinians proclaim as their own: the Palestine Liberation Organization. It has been said (correctly, in the present author's opinion) that

> ...significant numbers of Palestinians see no one else [but the P.L.O.] capable of delivering what they consider minimal demands: self-determination and a state or 'entity' of their own on the West Bank and Gaza Strip...[15]

This suggests that, if the P.L.O. entered the negotiating process with a chance of getting self-determination and a state at the end, Palestinians would support the move and would permit the P.L.O. to accept the compromises that would be involved.

This places a solution within Israel's grasp. For, even though the Israeli government would prefer not to deal with the P.L.O.,[16] Israel could achieve peace by demonstrating to the Palestinians that it is prepared to support not the pseudo-autonomy of the Israeli Plan but genuine Palestinian self-determination and, eventually, a Palestinian state, with acceptable guarantees for

Israel's security to be negotiated beforehand. Viewed in this light, the Israeli autonomy Plan is not only unproductive but positively counterproductive, if the Israeli government indeed wishes to negotiate a lasting peace settlement in the near future: Israel simply cannot reject the Palestinians' minimal demands and expect at the same time to find the genuine Palestinian leadership ready and able to compromise. Israel must choose.

That choice is made more urgent by the fact that over the past decade the P.L.O. has made great strides in establishing its claim to be the sole legitimate representative of the Palestinian people. The United Nations General Assembly's grant of 'observer status' to the P.L.O. in 1974 advanced this claim considerably. In the words of one scholar:

> It is clear that 'observer status' must denote some degree of international personality... As the P.L.O. is not a state, it would seem reasonable to classify it as a governmental authority with claims to represent a people not yet established as a territorial unit.[17]

But does this debatable status give the P.L.O. such a position that its legal commitments would run even against a later, regularly established, Palestinian government? And does this status confer a right to guide Palestinian self-determination? Neither of these questions can be answered without qualification in the affirmative.

International law recognizes, however, the status of government-in-exile[18] through which the P.L.O. could gain certain established benefits. As a government, the P.L.O. could claim *de jure* sovereign power[19] and could claim the right to exercise authority for Palestinian external relations.[20] As a government-in-exile, the P.L.O. would have the power to enter into treaty relationships,[21] although its obligations would have to be assumed explicitly or implicitly by the state which it would claim to represent.[22] Such an assumption could well take place through the mechanism of a general Palestinian plebiscite on choices freely negotiated and agreed upon by a Palestinian government-in-exile. The moral and political effects of using that procedure would be far more persuasive than mere acquiescence by a much-restricted and not fully representative self-governing authority. The latter's legitimacy would in any case be undermined by Israel's evident intention to prevent international supervision of the elections for the authority itself.[23] To the extent, however, that the authority's legitimacy is established, its role as a local administration could be complementary to that of the government-in-exile, so that the formation of that government would not necessarily conflict with the Camp David Framework on this point. The authority could under those circumstances even be represented in the government.

Furthermore, the very existence of a government-in-exile would begin to bring the Palestinian movement into that nexus of rights and duties by means of which international law regulates the behaviour of the recognized members of the international community. The creation of a Palestinian government-in-exile would thus be a positive development for the other parties to negotiations on the Palestinians' future.

The positive advantages for the Palestinians would be even greater. Creation of a government would send a clear signal to the Palestinians that their leaders were agreed on a common policy behind which all Palestinians everywhere could rally. The Palestinians would be seen to have given definitive expression to their resolve to attain independence not on sufferance but as a matter of national right. The message would go out to the world that the Palestinians were capable of taking their destiny into their own hands and exercising it responsibly and that Israel's refusal to deal with representative Palestinians was unjustified. In consequence, the P.L.O. claim on the support and good will of the international community would be greatly strengthened and the intransigence of Israel highlighted for the world to see.

But if the establishment of a government-in-exile would produce such generally positive effects, why has that step not already been taken? Such a move has, in fact, been considered in the past. After the joint Soviet-American Statement on the Middle East in October 1977, reports from Beirut suggested that a Palestinian government-in-exile could be declared within the week.[24] The plan was said to be that the government would be headed by a prominent figure from the West Bank or an independent Palestinian from outside the occupied territory and would include independent Palestinians as well as members of the P.L.O.[25] Nothing came of this, and objections were said to arise from a 'concern that such a step could provoke a power struggle in the movement which it could ill afford'.[26] The present author has heard similar misgivings from West Bank activists who fear that a Palestinian government would need to formulate specific policies on contentious issues and thereby tend to exclude those whose proposals were rejected.

These fears are not unfounded, given the political extremes within the Palestinian movement. But it is of the essence of responsible politics that even the bitterest differences, as in the Austrian case, should be submerged for the common good. It is much to be regretted that Israel's denial of Palestinian rights turned the Palestinian movement into one of 'armed struggle' in which a handful of die-hards might now hold out against the general consensus. While understanding the commitment of individual Palestinians to the use of force as the only answer to Israel's reliance on military power, one may nevertheless conclude that in the end violence must yield to statesmanship. There cannot be a stable and prosperous Palestinian state until this happens, and until such a state exists the Palestinian people will be denied the peaceful enjoyment of its national heritage. It must be said, furthermore, that the Palestinian claim to world sympathy and support would be considerably weakened if hopes for a general Middle East peace were frustrated primarily because the Palestinians could not get their own house in order.

But if the Palestinians do seize the initiative (and thereby pre-empt efforts by the other parties to choose tame Palestinian representatives[27]) peace negotiations could still be frustrated by Israeli refusal to deal with the Palestinian government. In the past, Israel has rejected negotiations with the P.L.O. with the argument that it was a terrorist organization committed to the destruction of Israel. The Palestinian government could correctly reply that legally it was not the P.L.O. and was not bound by previous declarations of the P.L.O. There is however a more fundamental and significant response to be made: namely, that Palestinian attitudes have themselves evolved in the past few years and are not necessarily hostile to an accommodation with Israel. For the present author's observations of the West Bank over a period of fifteen years suggest that the Palestinians have by and large come to accept the existence of an Israeli state even as they reject and combat Israeli domination of what little is left of their homeland. Indeed, Palestinians now openly think the unthinkable and envisage coexistence between Palestine and Israel.[28]

It is in this context that due regard should be given to the repeated indications by the Chairman of the Palestine Liberation

Organization of Palestinian readiness to accept the possibility of coexistence. In the late summer of 1977, Mr Arafat declared, in the context of an attempt by the Carter administration to bring the P.L.O. into the Geneva peace process, that the P.L.O. would agree to participate in negotiations on the basis of a revision of Security Council Resolution 242 which recognized both Israel's right to exist and the Palestinian right to an independent state.[29] The Camp David Framework, though going in some areas beyond the inadequate formulations of Resolution 242, did not meet this minimum Palestinian requirement, but Mr Arafat nevertheless significantly expanded the P.L.O. commitment to coexistence in discussions with Congressman Paul Findley in November 1978.[30] Mr Arafat's statements at that time deserve particular attention.

Chairman Arafat gave Congressman Findley this pledge of non-violence:

> The P.L.O. will accept an independent Palestinian state consisting of the West Bank and Gaza, with connecting corridor, and in that circumstance will renounce any and all violent means to enlarge the territory of that state. I would reserve the right, of course, to use non-violent means, that is to say diplomatic and democratic means to bring about the eventual unification of all of Palestine.[31]

In answer to the Congressman's questions, the Chairman declared: 'We will give *de facto* recognition to the State of Israel' and 'we would live at peace with all our neighbors'.[32] Mr Findley's conclusion from these statements was a fair one: 'Israel can no longer say that the P.L.O. is pledged to destroy Israel with force'.[33]

On that basis, even if it were proper to identify the position of the P.L.O. with that of a Palestinian government, such identification would not provide Israel with a valid excuse for refusing to negotiate.

Therefore, once the Palestinians had established the legal form of their representation through a government-in-exile, all parties could reasonably be expected to begin negotiating on the terms of a comprehensive peace between Israel and Palestine. We have seen that the Camp David Framework left two major points unresolved: the mechanism of full self-determination for the Palestinians and the solution of the refugee issue. The question at issue is: can these two aspects of the Palestinian problem be dealt with in such a way that Palestinians will agree to give guarantees of full security to Israel?

It has long been recognized that a massive programme of economic assistance would be an essential element in the consolidation of peace in order that, in the words of the Brookings Report, 'the state or entity in which Palestinian self-determination is realized ...[be enabled] to survive and develop'.[34] A number of countries, including Saudi Arabia (at least before its disenchantment with the Egyptian-Israeli Peace Treaty of March 1979), have been reported ready to contribute support for Middle East economic development.[35] Such economic aid may also provide the key to solution of the refugee problem. Repatriation or compensation has been the United Nations plan on this issue, and there is much to be said for the view that the more attractive the compensation, the fewer the Palestinians who will choose to return to what remains of their homes in Israel.[36] The Brookings plan proposes compensation in the context of making good the losses of Palestinian refugees from Israel and the losses of Jewish immigrants from Arab countries,[37] and, although equating the two groups might be objectionable in principle to the Arab side,[38] there does not as a practical matter seem to be any reason why the competing claims could not both be met. But there is clearly an element in the Palestinian case that does not apply to that of the Jewish emigrants. The latter left their Arab homes in order to exercise, either collectively or individually, their right of self-determination in a Jewish state, whereas the Palestinian exodus was in the context of a denial of self-determination. Compensation for the Palestinian refugees thus involves recompense not only for lost property but also in some sense for infringement of national rights and aspirations. That this was perpetrated not merely by Israel but by the international community as a whole acting through the League of Nations and the United Nations merely aggravates the Palestinian grievance. For the Palestinians there is therefore an important psychological element in the compensation question involving national pride and honour.

Major-General Chaim Herzog in his book on the war of October 1973, observes that (at least until that war) Israeli leaders had never understood the importance and significance of Arab pride, self-respect and honour.[39] Those leaders were not unique in this respect, and although the oversight may not be decisive in a state of military confrontation, it cannot be persisted in by any of the parties to a Middle East settlement if a peaceful relationship based on goodwill is to be established. The peace, to be successful, must in the end give the Palestinians a sense that their rights have been vindicated and reparation made for their suffering. Monetary compensation in such a situation has long been an accepted procedure in national courts in cases between individuals and on the international level in cases between states.[40] It is now time to apply it as between the international community and an injured people.

Once the issue of compensation is resolved, the peacemakers can consider how Palestinian self-determination may be related to security guarantees for Israel in such a way as not to infringe Palestinian sovereignty. Prof. Samir Anabtawi, himself of Palestinian origin, has emphasized the fundamental psychological element in Palestinian thinking on a state as fulfillment of self-determination:

> ...It's got to be a respectable state. It is not to be a state which is to be the object of ridicule among the Arab states or the Arab peoples and certainly not among the Palestinians themselves. There has to be a sense of pride in it, particularly in view of the fact that perhaps a number of Palestinians may elect not to go to such a state, but would nevertheless derive a certain measure of psychological comfort from its existence and from its capacity to perhaps extend its arm of protection to them if need be from time to time. There is the analogy perhaps in this regard between the Palestinians and a state of Palestine and world Jewry and Israel...[41]

Prof. Anabtawi went on to relate this psychological element to the practicalities of peace in a way which recalls the relevance of the Austrian experience:

> ...So if the Palestinian state must be respectable then it certainly must have the capacity for internal security...
> But there would be certain understandings: Such a state cannot wage an aggressive war, it cannot grant bases, it cannot follow really an aggressive foreign policy, it cannot have more than a certain number of troops or planes or what have you... [The state could acquiesce in this because it would receive in return] a guarantee of political independence and territorial integrity...a guarantee from the great powers, a guarantee from the Arab states, indeed a guarantee from Israel.
>
> ...I expect that such a state would ultimately emerge as a kind

147

of fulcrum for stability, where everybody has a stake in its maintenance...[42]

The example of the Austrian State Treaty demonstrates that restrictions on the composition and equipment of military forces are permissible even in the context of state sovereignty,[43] and Prof. Khalidi has indeed already detailed for the Palestinian armed forces levels of military strength[44] whose ratios to Israeli forces could be incorporated in the peace treaty. The question of foreign policy and bases is more complicated and on it the Austrian example suggests another major component of Middle East peace.

For the Austrian State Treaty does not itself impose neutrality on Austria. Rather that obligation was undertaken by Austria after it was given its independence by the Treaty, although the Austrian government under the occupation had before independence expressed its willingness to make the necessary declaration.[45] The purpose of this procedure was apparently to avoid the problem of Austria's 'neutralization' being taken as a lessening of her sovereignty. This explains the elucidation of Austria's position given several years later by then Foreign Minister Bruno Kreisky:

Actually, it is not accurate to speak of neutrality in peacetime, because what the term really means is non-participation in war. An attitude of indifference toward the ideological struggle has more properly been called neutralism (as opposed to neutrality). But this should not be taken to mean that neutrality does not impose any obligations whatever upon a country in peacetime. Such obligations can be summarized as follows:

1. A neutral country cannot join a military alliance in time of peace because in so doing it would destroy its ability to remain neutral in time of war.

2. Similarly, a neutral country must bar foreign military bases from its territory, since they would diminish its freedom of action – or, rather, non-action – in time of war.

3. A neutral country must not accept any obligations – political, economic or other – which would tend to impair its neutrality in wartime.

...the Austrian government has repeatedly stressed that neutrality, as far as Austria is concerned, is exclusively a matter of its own determination in accord with its own foreign and, of course, military policies.[46]

In short, neutrality was internally acceptable and externally feasible because a legitimate and representative Austrian government was willing, and was permitted, to demonstrate to its people and to the world that it was nobody's marionette.

The conclusion, then, is that international law can provide the means for accommodating divergent interests where there is a will towards accommodation. That will does exist among the Palestinians, even in their subjection, as the following statement by Mayor Milhem of Halhul implies:

> The Palestinian people are aware of the complexity of the issues. They certainly do not expect that the accumulated injustices will vanish overnight, and they do not daydream of easy and sudden freedom. But they are equally aware of the sterility of negotiating a settlement that in advance rules out the essence of their national identity, rights and aspirations.[47]

And the will is not absent in Israel. Former Foreign Minister Abba Eban has expressed the view that Israel should accept on the West Bank any regime that will not be hostile to Israeli security and he has proposed to his countrymen that 'we ought to be considering how Israel should rescue its basic interests, which are modest but crucial territorial change, demilitarization, military balance, mutual accessibility – those things which would make an Arab West Bank feasible for Israel'[48].

One can only hope that the voice of reason and moderation will, with the encouragement of the international community, and particularly of the European Economic Community and the United States, find receptive hearers.

NOTES

1　Assistant Secretary of State Harold Saunders in 78 DEPT. OF STATE BULLETIN (Nov. 1978) at 44.

2　The suggestion was made by Prof. Samir Anabtawi on May 24, 1977, in New York at a symposium whose speeches were published in pamphlet form as AMERICAN FRIENDS SERVICE COMMITTEE, CAN AN ISRAELI STATE AND A PALESTINIAN STATE CO-EXIST?

The idea was later picked up in Khalidi *Thinking the Unthinkable: a Sovereign Palestinian State*, 56 FOREIGN AFFAIRS 695–713.

On the resumption of Austrian independence, *see*

WHITEMAN, I DIGEST OF INTERNATIONAL LAW 348–355.

3 K. WALDHEIM, THE AUSTRIAN EXAMPLE 43–44, 47, 49–70 (1973).

4 *Id*. at 5 (international trend towards peaceful coexistence); at 59 (Austria's willingness to make financial sacrifices and accept neutrality to restore her sovereignty); at 89 (Austrian Chancellor's indication that neutrality was accepted willingly to ensure peace and prosperity for the country); at 83–87 (willingness of the Allied powers to accept that neutrality did not prevent an active Austrian role in the United Nations, although [*see* WHITEMAN, note 2 *supra*, at 350] some legal experts thought the two incompatible).
   See also BARKER, AUSTRIA 1918–1972, at 193–199.

5 BARKER, note 4 *supra*, at 173.

6 *Id*. 160, and cf. 162 on elections.

7 *Id*. 199.

8 *Id*. 164.

9 *Id*. 154.

10 *Id*. 153–154.

11 Austrian State Treaty, 6 U.S.T. 2369, T.I.A.S. No. 3298, 217 U.N.T.S. 223, in Article 1.

12 BARKER, note 4 *supra*, at 194, 196.

13 Austrian State Treaty, note 11 *supra*, Article 12 (prohibiting service of former Nazis in the Austrian military forces) and Article 16 (prohibiting Austrian purchase of German or Japanese military planes).

14 *See* article by Mayor Milhem of Halhul in NEWSWEEK, July 9, 1979, at 15.

15 N.Y. Times, Feb. 21, 1978 at 14, cols. 1–6.

16 Jerusalem Post Int'l Ed., June 28, 1977, at 5, col.1.

17 GREIG, INTERNATIONAL LAW 105 (2nd ed.).

18 BROWNLIE, PRINCIPLES OF PUBLIC INTERNATIONAL LAW 68 (3rd. ed.).

19 WHITEMAN, note 2 *supra*, at 921.

20 *Id*., at 922.

21 *Id*., at 926.

22 *Id*. 921.

23 *See*, Boston Globe, July 12, 1979, at 3, cols. 4–6.

24 N.Y. Times, Oct. 2, 1977, at 16, col.3.

25 *Id*.

26   *Id.*
27   Cf. comment of Milhem on this, note 14 *supra.*
28   *See* Khalidi, note 2 *supra.*
29   Jer. Post Int'l. Ed., Sept. 26, 1977, at 2, col.4.
30   *See* Findley press release 'Arafat Pledge Opens Door for U.S. Talks with P.L.O.' Washington, December 1, 1978.
31   *Id.*, at 3.
32   *Id.*, at 4.
33   *Id.*
34   TOWARD PEACE IN THE MIDDLE EAST, The Brookings Institution, 1975 (hereinafter THE BROOK-INGS REPORT) at 11.
35   Jer. Post Int'l. Ed., March 28, 1978, at 10, col.1.
36   Cf. Khalidi, note 2 *supra*, at 708.
37   THE BROOKINGS REPORT, note 34 *supra*, at 11.
38   Aside from legal arguments based on the unique position of the Palestinians as beneficiaries of United Nations calls for their repatriation (*see* CATTAN, PALESTINE AND INTERNATIONAL LAW 104–107), it may be argued that the Jewish emigrants from Arab countries lost personal, or perhaps community, property, while the Palestinians lost the economic infrastructure of a nation and thereby lost also the fruits of national economic development which accrued instead to Israel. *See* D. PERETZ, THE MIDDLE EAST TODAY 296 (2nd ed., 1971):
     'The Arabs continually point out that it was the loss by the refugees of their fields, orchards, vineyards, homes, shops, factories, and businesses that facilitated the incipient rapid growth of Israel. Of the first 370 Jewish settlements established after 1948, 350 were on former Arab property. Whole Arab cities – such as Jaffa, Acre, Lydda, Ramle, Baysan, and Majdal – 388 towns and villages, and large parts of others, containing nearly a quarter of all buildings standing in Israel during 1948, were abandoned by the refugees. Ten thousand shops, businesses, and stores were left in Jewish hands, as well as some 30,000 acres of citrus groves that supplied at least a quarter of the new state's foreign currency earnings.'
39   HERZOG, THE WAR OF ATONEMENT 13 (1975).
40   BROWNLIE, note 18 *supra*, 459–461.
41   Anabtawi, at the symposium noted at note 2 *supra.*

42 *Id.*
43 *See* note 13 *supra.*
44 *See* Khalidi, note 2 *supra*, at 703–704.
45 WALDHEIM, note 3 *supra*, at 68, the Moscow Memorandum of April 15, 1955 stated:
'…the Austrian federal government will make a declaration in a form that would impose upon Austria the international obligation always to observe a neutrality such as is observed by Switzerland…' The text of the Constitutional law embodying this undertaking is at WALDHEIM 78.
46 Quoted in WHITEMAN, note 2 *supra*, at 355.
47 Milhem, note 14 *supra.*
48 Quoted in editorial N.Y. Times, June 10, 1979, at 18E, cols. 1 & 2.

Appendix

The Begin Plan

SELF-RULE for Palestinian Arabs, Residents of Judea, Samaria, and the Gaza District, Which Will Be Instituted upon the Establishment of Peace –

[1]

The administration of the military government in Judea, Samaria and the Gaza district will be abolished.

[2]

In Judea, Samaria and the Gaza district, administrative autonomy of the residents, by and for them, will be established.

[3]

The residents of Judea, Samaria and the Gaza district will elect an administrative council composed of 11 members. The administrative council will operate in accordance with the principles laid down in this paper.

[4]

Any resident, 18 years old and above, without distinction of citizenship, or if stateless, is entitled to vote in the elections to the administrative council.

[5]

Any resident whose name is included in the list of candidates for the administrative council and who, on the day the list is submitted, is 25 years old or above, is entitled to be elected to the council.

[6]

The administrative council will be elected by general, direct, personal, equal and secret ballot.

[7]

The period of office of the administrative council will be four years from the day of its election.

[8]

The administrative council will sit in Bethlehem.

[9]

All the administrative affairs relating to the Arab residents of the areas of Judea, Samaria and the Gaza district, will be under the direction and within the competence of the administrative council.

[10]

The administrative council will operate the following departments: education; religious affairs; finance; transportation; construction and housing; industry, commerce and tourism; agriculture; health; labor and social welfare; rehabilitation of refugees; and the department for the administration of justice and the supervision of the local police forces, and promulgate regulations relating to the operations of these departments.

[11]

Security and public order in the areas of Judea, Samaria and the Gaza district will be the responsibility of the Israeli authorities.

[12]

The administrative council will elect its own chairman.

[13]

The first session of the administrative council will be convened 30 days after the publication of the election results.

[14]

Residents of Judea, Samaria and the Gaza district, without distinction of citizenship, or if stateless, will be granted free choice (option) of either Israeli or Jordanian citizenship.

[15]

A resident of the areas of Judea, Samaria and the Gaza district who requests Israeli citizenship will be granted such citizenship in accordance with the citizenship law of the state.

[16]

Residents of Judea, Samaria and the Gaza district who, in accordance with the right of free option, choose Israeli citizenship, will be entitled to vote for, and be elected to, the Knesset in accordance with the election law.

[17]

Residents of Judea, Samaria and the Gaza district who are citizens of Jordan or who, in accordance with the right of free option will become citizens of Jordan, will elect and be eligible for election to the Parliament of the Hashemite Kingdom of Jordan in accordance with the election law of that country.

[18]

Questions arising from the vote to the Jordanian Parliament by residents of Judea, Samaria and the Gaza district will be clarified in negotiations between Israel and Jordan.

[19]

A committee will be established of representatives of Israel, Jordan and the administrative council to examine existing legislation in Judea, Samaria and the Gaza district and to determine which legislation will continue in force, which will be abolished and what will be the competence of the administrative council to promulgate regulations. The rulings of the committee will be adopted by unanimous decisions.

[20]

Residents of Israel will be entitled to acquire land and settle in the areas of Judea, Samaria and the Gaza district. Arabs, residents of Judea, Samaria and the Gaza district who, in accordance with the free options granted them, will become Israeli citizens, will be entitled to acquire land and settle in Israel.

[21]

A committee will be established of representatives of Israel, Jordan and the administrative council to determine norms of immigration to the areas of Judea, Samaria and the Gaza district. The committee will determine the norms whereby Arab refugees residing outside Judea, Samaria and the Gaza district will be permitted to immigrate to these areas in reasonable numbers. The ruling of the committee will be adopted by unanimous decision.

[22]

Residents of Israel and residents of Judea, Samaria and the Gaza district will be assured of movement and freedom of economic activity in Israel, Judea, Samaria and the Gaza district.

[23]

The administrative council will appoint one of its members to represent the council before the Government of Israel for

155

deliberation on matters of common interest, and one of its members to represent the council before the Government of Jordan for deliberation on matters of common interest.

[24]

Israel stands by its right and its claim of sovereignty to Judea, Samaria and the Gaza district. In the knowledge that other claims exist, it proposes, for the sake of the agreement and the peace, that the question of sovereignty be left open.

[25]

With regard to the administration of the holy places of the three religions in Jerusalem, a special proposal will be drawn up and submitted that will include the guarantee of freedom of access to members of all faiths to the shrines holy to them.

[26]

These principles will be subject to review after a five-year period.

NOTE

The above text is based on that said to be the official English version as published in the *New York Times*, Dec. 29, 1977, city ed., p.A8, cols 1–3. That version has been compared with a text said to be that read out in the Knesset by Prime Minister Begin and published in the *Jerusalem Post* International Edition, January 3, 1978, p.10, cols 2–3.

Generally, spelling, capitalization, and punctuation as in the *New York Times* text have been followed here, with the following alterations based on the *Jerusalem Post* text:

– In Article 10 semi-colons have been substituted for commas in order to indicate more clearly the duties assigned to each department;

– in Article 16 a comma has been added after the words 'elected to';

– in Article 23 a semi-colon was changed to a comma;

– in Article 24 a comma was added after 'purposes'.

Major textual differences between the two texts are in Article 4 (a matter of translation) and Article 24 whose final clause in the *Jerusalem Post* version reads: 'that the question of sovereignty in these areas be left open'. The *New York Times* version has been followed in both instances.

The heading 'SELF-RULE...Establishment of Peace' was omitted from the *New York Times* version and is reproduced here from the text in the *Jerusalem Post*.

The numbering of Article 6 was omitted from the *New York Times* text and is taken from the version in the *Jerusalem Post*.